AMERICAN WOMEN

images and realities

AMERICAN WOMEN
Images and Realities

Advisory Editors
ANNETTE K. BAXTER
LEON STEIN

A Note About This Volume

Little is known about Salome Lincoln Mowry (1807-1841) before May 1829 when, with her co-workers, she joined in a strike against a wage cut at the New England mill where they were employed. But when the others, no longer able to endure, returned to work, Salome Lincoln parted company with them and journeyed from town to town throughout New England, spreading the word that in the eyes of the Lord all were equal, and that women as well as men had the right to speak forth.

THE

FEMALE PREACHER,

OR

MEMOIR OF

SALOME LINCOLN

By
ALMOND H. DAVIS

ARNO PRESS

A New York Times Company

New York • 1972

Reprint Edition 1972 by Arno Press Inc.

American Women: Images and Realities
ISBN for complete set: 0-405-04445-3
See last pages of this volume for titles.

Manufactured in the United States of America

- - - - - - - - - - - - - -

Library of Congress Cataloging in Publication Data

Davis, Almond H
   The female preacher.

   (American women: images and realities)
   1. Mowry, Salome Lincoln, 1807-1841   I. Title.
II. Series.
BR1725.M68D38 1972   253'.2'0924 [B]   72-2599
ISBN 0-405-04489-5

THE

FEMALE PREACHER

Salome Lincoln

Math. 25: 6. "Behold the Bridegroom cometh".   Page 46. 47

This book was thine - here didst thou read -   This picture, oh! yes here
indeed I see thee still.

Thayer & Co. Lith. Boston

THE

FEMALE PREACHER,

OR

MEMOIR OF

SALOME LINCOLN,

AFTERWARDS THE WIFE OF

ELDER JUNIA S. MOWRY.

By
ALMOND H. DAVIS.

"The righteous shall be in everlasting remembrance."

PSALMS CXII.: 6.

PROVIDENCE:
PUBLISHED BY ELDER J. S. MOWRY,
AT THE BOOKSTORE OF ISAAC WILCOX, 5 MARKET SQUARE.
BOSTON:
FOR SALE BY D. S. KING AND CO., NO. 1 CORNHILL.
1843.

BOSTON:

PRINTED BY A. B. KIDDER, 7 CORNHILL.

PREFACE,

———◆———

"COURTEOUS READER!—While such a mass of books at the present day, are being published in so cheap a manner, and the tendency of many of them, being to *corrupt* the public mind, it becomes the duty of the christian community, to use every means to counteract their influence.

"It was while watching with her, during her last moments, that it occurred to me, that a short sketch of her life and trials, might be a benefit to others by placing in the hands of the public, *facts* rather than FICTION. And in the language of another,—

"The Memorials of the good, constitute one of the most sacred possessions of the church of Christ. It is not submitted to our choice, whether or not, we will preserve and hand down the character of such as have been eminent in their day, for the savor and strength of their piety—the ardor and steadfastness of their devotion, the consistency and power of their example, and the abundance and success of their labors in the cause of their Crucified King. There is a moral obligation, resting on each successive generation of her children, to perpetuate *these* LIVING *evidences of Christianity*."

" At the time I placed her papers in the hands of the Author, I had but a faint idea of publishing her Memoir. But the additional amount of matter collected—and the many interesting facts, embodied, all conspired to increase the conviction that such a work would be highly valuable to the public. But what finally led me to decide in favor of this step was, that I might be more extensively useful, by causing to be placed in the hands of the reader, a '*written monument*,' that will preach after I am laid in the dust with her. These are my only motives in publishing this work; and if these records of my beloved companion, and fellow laborer in the gospel, shall be instrumental in awakening one impenitent sinner, or of stirring up the minds of any to greater usefulness, I shall rejoice, and my object will have been accomplished. I conclude in the prayer of another,—' Hand it, O my Savior, to dying men and women, with a blessing from above.' "

J. S. MOWRY.

Smithfield, R. I., May 9th, 1843.

CONTENTS.

INTRODUCTION.

CHAPTER I.

YOUTH.

CHAPTER II.

A CALL TO PREACH.

CHAPTER III.

MISCELLANEOUS.

CHAPTER IV.

THE FEMALE PREACHER.

CHAPTER V.

THE FEMALE PREACHER

Continued.

CHAPTER VI.

THE FEMALE PREACHER.

Concluded.

CHAPTER VII.

THE WIFE.

CHAPTER VIII.

THE LAST SICKNESS.

INTRODUCTION.

~~~~~~~

"While thus within, contending armies strove,
Without, the christian had his trials too."—*Pollok*.

APOLOGY FOR THIS WORK. I am aware, that
female preaching at the present day, among a large
and respectable body of christians, has become very
unpopular. But this is no reason why we should
keep silent. Many things which are rejected by the
world, are undoubtedly approved by God. Vital
christianity, is unpopular; as but few embrace its
principles, and if an individual would become a
truly devoted christian, in the sight of God, he must
at the same time, lose the popular favor of the
world. But is this a sufficient reason why the minister of the gospel, who believes in holiness of heart,
should keep silent? On the other hand, is it not the
very reason why he should CRY ALOUD against every
sin, *and spare not ?*

From these remarks, the reader will perceive, that
the author of this work, has not written, expecting to
gain the popular favor of the world, but from a strong
conviction of right; and if by thus doing, he can

2

promote the cause of virtue and holiness, he will have accomplished all he desires, and the world may regard his labors as they choose.

MANNER OF COLLECTING THE FACTS:—Soon after the death of Mrs. Mowry, her husband, together with some other friends, were desirous that her life should appear before the public. And at their urgent request, the author undertook the task of preparing it for the press:—a task, for which, he feels himself but poorly qualified.

At her death, Sister Mowry left a Journal of about thirty pages, and that, written during a period of but little importance in her history. Besides this she left nearly, if not quite, one hundred letters, from different individuals. These too, contained but few facts relative to her. Under these considerations, we concluded to visit the different places where she had labored, and collect what facts we could, and the letters written by herself.—We collected about fifty, together with many more interesting incidents. And from these, together with her journal, we were able to trace her history, from birth to death.

From the manner her journal has been collected, it would not be surprising if the reader should find some errors; especially among the dates. Should this be the case, we trust the above explanation will serve as an apology.

REASONS WHY MRS. MOWRY ENTERED THE FIELD OF LABOR, AS A PREACHER OF THE GOSPEL.—It could not have been a love of gain, that prompted

Sister Mowry to go out from home, as a public speaker; as her labors in the gospel field never supported her, neither did she expect it. It was not from a love of ease, as she knew something of the hardships attending such a course, even before she engaged. Neither was it from a love of self-aggrandizement; as she well knew, from the example of those who had preceded her, that she must certainly meet with the slander, and bitter reproach of the world. This is somewhat peculiar to all devoted christians, but especially *Female Preachers*. Pollok in speaking of the slander and reproach heaped upon the christian, says :—

> " And slander, worse than mockery, or sword,
> Or death, stood nightly at her horrid forge,
> And fabricated lies, to stain his name,
> And wound his peace. "

Christ says, — "If ye were of the world, the world would love his own; but because ye are not of the world, but I have chosen you out of the world, therefore the world hateth you." — *St. John* **15 : 19.**— But in the language of the poet,

> * * * Still she had a source
> Of happiness, that men could neither give
> Nor take away : *The Avenue* that led
> To IMMORTALITY before her lay. "

I firmly believe, all that ever prompted Mrs. Mowry to take the stand she did, was a deep rooted conviction, like Paul; that, — "Woe is to me, *if* I PREACH not the gospel."

OBJECTIONS TO FEMALE PREACHERS: It is advocated with considerable warmth, that woman is acting out of her sphere, when she takes a part in the public congregation. I once, from a prejudice early imbibed, without searching for the "thus saith the Lord," maintained the same views. But whatever may have been my former opinion, I am now satisfied, that God's ways are not as our ways; and he will choose just such agents to execute his plans, as best subserves his ends. And when he has chosen them, he will give them an evidence, that they are his servants. And if Mrs. Mowry did not have this, we can gain no evidence that any individual has, since the days of the apostles.

The principal objection to female speaking in public, arises from early prejudice. And in fact one author in a recent article on this subject, speaking of 1 Cor. xiv. 34, 35, says — "Having been familiar with these passages from my youth, I have never doubted for a moment, the unscripturalness and impropriety of females becoming public exhorters, teachers and speakers. —" It is somewhat remarkable that whenever this subject is introduced, the objector always resorts to the Fourteenth chapter of 1 Corinthians, — as though there were no other passage in scripture, of sufficient strength to meet their preconceived notions. But as we shall soon have occasion to refer to that, we will leave it for the present.

Another objection to female preaching, is, that

it would be improper for women to become pastors. It is not my intention, to advocate *Female Pastors;* but a woman may express her views in public, by way of exhortation &c.;—without taking upon herself the care of a church. As in the days of the apostles, there were different gifts in the church, so it is at the present day. "Now there are diversities of gifts, but the same spirit; And there are differences of administration, but the same Lord. * * * For to one is given by the spirit, the *word of wisdom,* to another, the word of *knowledge* by the same spirit; To another, *faith* by the same spirit; To another, the *gift of healing* by the same spirit; To another, the *working of miracles;* to another, PROPHECY; to another, *discerning of spirits;* to another, divers kinds of tongues, to another, interpretation of tongues:"— 1 Cor. xii. 4, 5, 8, 9, 10.

But some who admit the propriety of women speaking in public conference, deny them the right of going into the pulpit, and taking a text for the foundation of remarks: but I have yet to learn, that the pulpit is a more sacred place, than any other portion of the house. And if it is right for woman to speak in public conference, it is right for her to quote passages of scripture, and if right to quote scripture, it is also right to take a passage as the foundation of remarks; and as the desk is not the *sanctum sanctorum* of God's house, it is equally right to enter that—with a text selected from the word of God.

But the strongest objection in the minds of many,

2*

is "*It is* UNPOPULAR." Says the same author to whom
we have just alluded : — "As to the usages of the
Baptist churches, permit me to say, that in England
such a practise is not known, and would not be tol-
erated." He also refers to the Middle States of
this country. But had he referred to the apostolic
dispensation instead of those places, I think the
argument would have been better grounded. But
leaving this part of the subject; I now proceed to
notice the objection raised from the Epistle of Paul
to the Corinthians.

"LET YOUR WOMEN KEEP SILENCE IN THE CHUR-
CHES," &c. 1 Cor. xiv. 34. The subject of female
preaching, can scarcely be introduced, but what this
oft repeated passage is rehearsed. But that we may
be mistaken in Paul's meaning, is not impossible.
Dr. Clark remarks in his comments on this verse ; —
"This was a Jewish ordinance. Women were not
permitted to teach in their assemblies, or even to ask
questions. The Rabbies taught, that *woman*, should
know nothing but the use of *her distaff.*"

The same doctrine is extensively taught, among
all the barbarous nations at the present day. But
the sentiment, savors too much of oppression, to be
advocated in this enlightened age. And again it
should be remembered, that it is the doctrine of
men, and not of God—It lays no claim to Divine
Inspiration. Rabbi Elezar also remarks, "Let the
words of the *Law* be BURNED, rather than that they
should be delivered to woman." But where is the

christian, that would be willing now to embrace this sentiment.

That the apostle did not mean to preclude woman from speaking in public, is self evident, when we take into consideration his remarks on other occasions. " But every woman that prayeth or prophesieth with her head uncovered dishonoreth her head," &c. — 1 Cor. xi. 5. Says Dr. Clark, "Whatever may be the meaning of praying or prophesying in respect to the man: they have precisely the same meaning in respect to the woman; so that women, at least as well as some men, might speak to others, to edification, exhortation and comfort. "

The apostle in making the remark, which he did in the fourteenth chapter of Corinthians, instead of intending to prohibit Pious Females from speaking for the edification of others, alluded to the confusion which frequently occurred in the churches, by the troublesome asking of questions; and probably women, as well as men frequently annoyed them in this way. This is evident from the three preceding verses, commencing at the 31st—" For ye may ALL prophesy, one by one, that all may learn, and all be comforted ? 33 verse. For God is not the author of confusion, but of peace, as in all churches of the saints. " * —Then comes the words under consideration : — "Let your women keep silence in the churches, for it is not permitted unto them to speak ; but

* See also : — II Timothy ii. 23. Titus iii. 9.

they are commanded to be under obedience, as also saith the law.

WOMEN DID PROPHESY, OR PREACH IN THE TIME OF CHRIST AND THE APOSTLES; AND WERE APPROVED. The term prophesy in scripture, as generally used is nearly synonymous with the term preaching as understood at the present day. The term prophesy — signifies explaining scripture, speaking to the church in public, by way of exhortation, singing the praises of God, in the language of inspiration, or foretelling future events. * That prophesying and exhortation, or preaching, was understood by the apostle to mean the same, is evident from his words in 1 Cor. xiv. 3. — "But he that *Prophesyeth*, speaketh unto men to edification, and exhortation, and comfort." Again the Revelator declares that the testimony of Jesus is the spirit of Prophesy.— Rev. xix. 10.

That women were to prophesy is evident from Joel xi. 28 verse, — "And it shall come to pass afterwards, that I will pour out my spirit upon all flesh ; and your sons, and your DAUGHTERS shall prophesy, &c. "

Here we see that the spirit of prophesy, was to be poured out upon woman, as well as man : And that WOMEN did *Prophesy* or *Preach* in the time of Christ and his apostles is still more evident. Mariam and Deborah prophesied. And the Prophetess Anna,

* See Encyclopedia of Religious knowledge — Article Prophet.

bore testimony at the coming of Christ, as well as Simeon. The apostle was aware that women prophesied ; For the sacred penman tells us : — Acts xxi. 8, 9. And the next day we that were of PAUL's company, departed and came into Ceserea; and we entered the house of Philip the Evangelist, which was one of the seven, and abode with him. And the same man had *Four* DAUGHTERS, virgins, which did PROPHESY.

No comment need be made upon these last references. And I will close by simply adding, that Aquila, and Priscilla, expounded the law unto Apollos, who himself, was an eloquent man, and mighty in scripture. Acts xviii. 24–26 — Many other quotations might be made, to show that women did actually speak in public, in the days of the primitive church. But enough we think has already been cited ; therefore I will desist.

It was woman that preached Christ to the Samaritans, after she had learned of him, at Jacob's well ! —

It was woman that first preached a risen Savior ! and shame on that man, who will take advantage of the apostle's meaning, in the fourteenth of Corinthians, by construing it into something he never intended ; in order to make her condition still more degraded.

A. H. DAVIS.

Boston, April 28, 1843.

MEMOIR.

CHAPTER I.

YOUTH.

> " We spend
> A ten years' breath,
> Before we apprehend,
> What 'tis to live or fear a death."

YOUTH, in many respects, is the happiest period of life. It is then, that the mind, unburdened with care, is left free to rove ; and like the bee to pluck her sweets from every flower. But as we advance onward up life's steep declivity, ere we are aware, we are immersed in the busy scenes of the world, and we can hardly tell why we live, or what is to be the ultimate object of our existence. But one thing is certain, we do not exist in vain, if we fulfil the design of our creation ;

which is, to spend the passing time in such a manner, as not only to benefit the world by our having lived in it ; but also to prepare for another, and a better. But how many there are, who have spent not only ten years, but a whole life — three score and ten ; and died, as the fool dieth, without knowing why they have lived, or what good they have accomplished. And on the other hand, how many, who have been truly useful in society, have died comparatively in obscurity. And hence it should be the object of the memorialist, to seek out such, that their virtues, and their names may be perpetuated among the living, for the benefit of coming generations.

SALOME LINCOLN, * —the daughter of Ambrose and Susanna Lincoln, was born at Raynham, Mass. in Bristol County, September 13, 1807. She was the eldest of six children ; only two of which are now living. Her father's residence, where she was born, is situated in the edge of Raynham, about five miles north of Taunton Green.

Her father was born in Taunton in 1784.

* We have thought proper to use her maiden name until the time when we shall speak of her marriage ; as many of the readers know her only by that.

Her mother, Susanna Weston, was born in Middleborough, Mass., in the year 1782.— They are both professors of religion : Her father having made a public profession, and united with the Christian Baptist Church in 1806 ; and her mother, in 1805 united with the Calvinist Baptist Church at Taunton. She afterwards took up her connection, and united with the Free Will Baptist, at Taunton, where she now remains.

PERSONAL APPEARANCE. In describing the person of Salome, I shall be forced to confine myself to the testimony of others, having never seen her myself. And the description, will better answer to her in after life, than in youth. Sister Lincoln in after life, say those who were acquainted with her, was above the middle size. Her hair was black — her eyes, dark and piercing, with an expression of mildness, and her features beamed with intelligence. In her dress, she was plain, yet tasty, and always manifested an excellent judgment in selecting the colors. She was not extravagant ; but dressed in a manner becoming her station. In early life however, before restrained by the influence of religion, she was naturally inclined to gay-

3

ety ; but after experiencing a change of heart she overcame those propensities.

Her voice was deep toned and heavy, and well suited to a public speaker. She sometimes spoke in large houses, and even in the open air ; and was distinctly heard by large audiences. " Her manner of speaking "—says one who often heard her, "was self-collected, and yet pathetic; simple, yet deep in thought." When she spoke in public, her feelings usually were engaged in the subject ; and with a soul yearning for the salvation of others, her words would sometimes fall upon the ears of the audience with a power almost irresistible ! Says an individual, who was intimate with her ; " Such exhortations and prayers, are not often heard, as proceeded from her lips. I shall never forget following her in prayer : She had addressed the throne of grace, in her peculiarly solemn and impressive manner, when I immediately followed ; but the contrast was so great, that I seemed in my own estimation, to have dwindled to the size of an infant. " In the pulpit her appearance was bold and commanding. She used but few jestures, but her manner was such as to gain the attention and interest of those who heard.

PRIVATE CHARACTER. It is the invariable
testimony of a large circle of acquaintance,
that Salome Lincoln maintained an excellent
character through life. But being reserved
in her manners, especially among strangers,
she sometimes drew forth the suspicions, if not
the enmity of those who knew her not. This
trait of character was natural to her from
childhood, and she did not entirely over-
come it. But to those of her familiar acquaintance, and who had gained her confidence, she was a faithful and tried friend.
There are several instances of this kind, of
a marked character, which we shall hereafter
notice.

Salome was naturally mild and amiable in
her temper — ready to yield even her own
rights for the sake of maintaining peace. —
Says her mother : — "I never knew her to
strike any one of her playmates, except in
one instance, and then she did not seem to be
in anger. " She was playing school, as children term it ; a play for which they seem to
be strikingly fond, as it gives them an opportunity to assume authority — and children, as
well as men, sometimes like to command,
and be obeyed. But it seems in this in-

stance, the boy over whom she usurped authority, did not prove a very obedient scholar.
And for his obstinacy, she did, what teachers sometimes have to do, to scholars of a
similar character.

CHRISTIAN CHARACTER. Sister Lincoln,
was a devoted christian ! She was not satisfied with an empty profession — that which
satisfies the world ! but she sought to be holy
in the sight of God. It is of but little importance how the world regard us ; if our hearts
are right ! — In her whole intercourse with
society, her conduct evinced a purity of heart,
a sincerity of action, strength of faith, and
warmth of christian love. These remarks
will apply to the latter part of her life with
force — but to say she sustained this character through every period, would perhaps be
saying more than is strictly true ; as a short
period passed, according to her own relation ;
and as we shall soon show, when she was in
what is commonly termed a backslidden state ;
but with the exception of this, the remarks
will apply with emphasis to her christian character, from the time of her conversion, until
her death. Says one who was familiar with
her from childhood, — "Such has been my

situation in life as to enable me to form many happy associations, with a large number of devoted christians ; and for a rigid adherence to principle — a uniform and consistent christian life, I must pronounce her one of the first ! It is not too much I think, to say that none among us stood higher in the estimation of the community, for talents and piety, than Salome. "

Religion, was her only theme. And she seems to have had a longing desire to become more and more transformed into the image of her Savior. After a careful examination of a large number of her letters, written to different individuals, we have not found one in which she has not mentioned the subject of religion. In one of these she says :— " Religion is the one thing needful !—I do not know of anything in this world I could put in the balance against RELIGION ! But O, — I want to be more and more rooted and grounded in the Lord ! " In another letter she says, — " How good *this religion* is ! Truly I receive an hundred fold in this life ; and am expecting Life Eternal in the world to come. "

It was religion that sustained her in her

3*

arduous labors for the salvation of her fellow-men! It was religion, that supported her through all her trials! It comforted her in sickness — It soothed her in death — And she is now enjoying its blissful influence among the ransomed millions in heaven! — O, blessed thought! — O, glorious immortality! —Who then would not be a christian ?

EDUCATION. Salome's advantages for acquiring an education were but limited, being confined to a common school. And common schools at the period when she attended, did not afford the facilities which are now offered, for rapid advancement. For the march of time has brought its improvements in this department, as well as in others. This to anxious parents, who are now forced to send their children abroad — unguarded, save by the watch-care of strangers, must be a source of satisfaction ; as they may look forward to the time as not far distant, when they can obtain an education at home, sufficient for all the business transactions of life.

Though Salome's advantages for obtaining an education, were limited, yet she did not misspend her time. She embraced every opportunity for improvement ; and by reading, and other means, she had by the time of her death, acquired a large store of useful knowledge; and gave an evidence to those around her, that her mind was highly cultivated. She spent much time in reading and meditation. Says Elder Johnson, — "Salome gathered books around her! and the time others spent in *gossiping* and *idle chit chat*, she spent in reading her Bible, and other books. Pursuing this course, she became retiring in her manners, and less social with those around her, unless it were on religious topics, and then very sparingly, conversing apparently, only when she hoped to get or do good."

EARLY HISTORY. Except some few facts which have been gathered from her writings, and from her friends, but little of importance is known of Salome, until she was fifteen years of age. Her mind was early led to the subject of religion, and to this fact undoubtedly she owes the formation of the character which she sustained in after life.

"As the twig is bent, the tree inclines."

is a maxim, which ought to be painted in large capitals, in the sitting room of every mother. Children may be taught virtue, as readily as vice. Mothers look to your children! If you neglect to teach them virtue, they will certainly learn vice.* But to return; Salome was early taught the existence of God, and the necessity of a preparation of heart, to meet him in peace.

EXPERIENCE. At the age of thirteen her mind was called to the subject of religion. This was sometime in the year 1820. Previous to this, according to her own relation, she had had many serious thoughts, when she reflected that she must meet a righteous God in judgment; and there render an account for all the deeds done in the body. When alone, she says — "I have often wept bitterly, wishing that I was prepared for death." But like many others under like circumstances, she said to the Holy Spirit; "Go thy way for this time, and when I have a more convenient season I will call for thee."

From this time, until 1822, her mind seemed to be wavering, and in doubt. Sometimes we find her earnestly seeking for the salva-

* Jeremy Taylor once said to a mother. "Madam! be at pains to educate your son, or be assured SATAN *will do it for you.*"

tion of her soul, and at others, among her friends at Middleborough, joining with her young companions in the vanities of the world, afraid to acknowledge her need of a Savior, through fear of their derision. She continued in this situation until she was FIFTEEN years of age, when she boldly determined to forsake all, and follow Christ.

She experienced religion sometime in the year 1822. She was then probably at work at Hopewell, a factory village in Taunton, about one mile from the Court House. It was soon after her return from a visit to her friends at Middleborough, Mass. As the relation of her experience is interesting, I will give it *verbatim* as recorded in her journal.

She says: — "I had now returned home, and determined that I would seek the Lord at the loss of all things. But the more I sought, the more I saw the wretchedness of my situation. I attended on the preaching of the gospel, but every word was like a thunderbolt to my wounded soul ! I felt that I was justly condemned, and despaired of the mercy of God. Once as the preacher came down from the desk, he requested those that desired prayers to come forward to the anx-

ious seats.   While he was praying, I rushed
from the seat where I was sitting, and knelt
with those who had already come forward.
I thought I had now given up my good name
and come out from the world; but still I
found no relief.   One day as I retired to a
small grove near the house, and sat down
under a large tree to meditate upon my lost
condition without Christ; it seemed to me
as though the heavens were brass, and the
earth was iron under my feet.   O! thought
I — I have lived but a few years! but I have
become a burden to myself! I felt that I had
sinned away the day of grace, and driven
the heavenly messenger from my breast!—
While I sat thus meditating; a thought like
this, came to my mind.   Has not Christ died
for the very worst of sinners? I cannot be
worse than the worst — perhaps there is yet
mercy for *me!*   I will cast myself upon him;
and if I die, I will die pleading — I then
threw myself upon my knees, and began to
cry: — O, Jesus — If thou wilt, thou canst
make me clean! While praying, it seemed
as though the mountains had rolled away,
and I heard these words:— "I will, be thou
clean!" My fears subsided.   The throbbings

of my bosom ceased; and a heavenly calm ensued. O, thought I, is it possible, I have found favor with God? I then arose and went towards the house; but Satan soon suggested to my mind, that I had only lost my conviction, and mistaken it for conversion. And now my case if possible, was even worse than before. Again I fell upon my knees, and besought the Lord, that if I had not found forgiveness, to give me an evidence; and then these words were sweetly applied to my mind: —

"Be not faithless, but believing."

O, what glory filled my soul at that moment! I arose, and every thing looked new around me! Every thing seemed to praise the Lord! and I longed to tell the whole world, what a DEAR SAVIOR I had found. I knew then, that he had taken my feet from the miry clay; and had set them upon the ROCK, even the *Rock* CHRIST JESUS!"

BAPTISM. April 8, 1823, Salome with nine others went forward in the ordinance of baptism. The rite was administered by Elder Ruben Allen, a Freewill Baptist minister then laboring with the church at Taunton.

In speaking of the ordinance she says:—

"It was a happy day to me. The banks were thronged with a large concourse of people, who had assembled to witness the administration. But my soul was so filled with the love of God, that I did not fear them. I could say in the language of the Poet :—

> "Blest be my God that I was born,
>   To hear the Gospel sound;
> That I was born, to be baptized,
>   When Gospel truths abound."

UNITES WITH THE CHURCH. In the month of July following her baptism, she was received, and united with the F. W. Baptist Church at Raynham. This church was a branch of the church at Taunton, and was under the pastoral charge of Elder H. N. Loring.

Though Salome gained so good an evidence of her acceptance with God, and as confident as others might have been that she would have remained steadfast; yet we are obliged to record a short period of her life, after her conversion, when she was without the enjoyment of religion. In speaking of it herself, she says — "The church began to decline, and I with the rest."

She remained in a backslidden state until sometime in the year 1825; when she was again reclaimed and brought back to her first love. This was during a powerful revival of religion in Raynham and the vicinity where she was then laboring.

The cause of her backsliding, she attributes to a neglect of duty. From the time of her conversion, it was deeply impressed upon her mind, that God had something for her to do as a public laborer in his vineyard.

A neglect of duty, is the usual cause of all backsliding. When the young convert begins to trust in his own strength, and like Peter, to walk the untrodden deep, he is sure to sink. But as long as he will draw nigh unto God, God will draw nigh unto him. And as long as he will walk in the paths God has marked out, his soul will prosper.

CHAPTER II.

A CALL TO PREACH.

" Woe is unto me if I *preach* not the Gospel. "—*Paul.*

"Go then earthly fame and treasure—
Come disaster, scorn and pain,
In THY service, pain is pleasure,
With THY favor loss is gain ! "

" A CALL to preach ! " says the reader — What! a WOMAN called to preach ? — Truly this is something new !

But stop my dear Sir! — let us reason for a moment.   What is a call to preach ?

The strongest evidence I can name, that an individual is called to preach the gospel, is, a deep conviction that it is his duty — this conviction being from God.   The apostle explains the nature of this call, when he says : — " For though I preach the gospel, I have nothing to glory of, for necessity is laid upon me; yea, WOE *is unto me*, if I *preach* not the gospel. " — 1 Cor. ix. 16.

This is one of the evidences, but there are others, and I will proceed to name them.

1. An individual called to preach the gospel, will feel to weep over sin, in high, as well as low places; and to do all he or she can, to promote the salvation of others.

2. "A call to preach, requires of the individual, a holy, blameless life, and abilities suited to the work ; such as knowledge, aptness to teach, courage, &c.—and an opportunity afforded in providence to be useful." *

These are some of the most prominent points, which we consider constitute a call to preach. Now if a woman has all these qualifications ; and there is no prohibition in the word of God, † may she not strictly be said to have a call from God to preach the gospel ?

The greatest difficulty at the present day, is, that too many preachers, have no higher call than of men. If more were called of God, and less of men, it would be better for the church, and better for the world.

Whether Sister Lincoln had the qualifications which I have named, or not, I leave for the reader to judge, after he shall have read her convictions, and the testimony of others.

* Prof. Knowles' Premium Tract.

† See Introduction, Page 14.

One thing, however, is certain, if she erred, she erred conscientiously.

It was early evident to the friends of Salome, from her striking gift in exhortation, that she was destined to fill a more conspicuous place in the church, and in society. And although her mind was strongly exercised on this subject, yet it was a long time before she yielded to a sense of duty, and took up her cross.

Her trials of mind, in relation to preaching, as we may naturally suppose, were severe. Situated as she was in a community, where female preachers were but little known : — and where the tide of popular favor was turned against them—with but limited means, without many friends to encourage her on, — while the spirit of God, and the convictions of conscience, said, go, go ! —and on the other hand, Satan, and the world, cried *Woman*, — woman ! — it is no wonder, that at the midnight hour, while she wept and prayed till her pillow was wet with tears; * she should sometimes exclaim, " Lord I pray thee, have me excused ! "

* It is related by her friends, that so great was her anxiety of mind on the subject of preaching, that she would often weep hours, after she had retired.

According to her own relation, her mind was first exercised on the subject of preaching, about the year 1823, soon after she united with the church.   In a letter addressed to a friend, she says ; — " I was employed in the weaving-room at Taunton. — My mind had often been exercised, in relation to entering the vineyard of the Lord, as a public laborer.   But, O, my soul shrunk from the work ! I thought I could never move forward ; and soon lost the enjoyment of religion. "

In another letter she says : — " I felt that it was a great undertaking ; and it was with a trembling hand, that I came to the conclusion to give up all, and enter the field.   But on making up my mind, I felt the approbation of heaven, and since then, I have been more and more convinced, that these convictions were from the Lord ! "

In remarking to a friend, she said, that it did not seem right to her, for a woman to speak in public ; and on account of this, like Jonah, she had fled from the presence of the Lord, to get rid of duty.   This impression was undoubtedly founded on the belief of others.   But one eminent writer, (Dr. Watts,) remarks, that truth is to be re-

4*

ceived, come from what source it may.   And
the truth of God is no less precious, because
it is spoken by woman; though the world
may claim dominion over her, and attempt to
seal her lips in perpetual silence.

Elder Lorenzo Johnson in speaking of her
call to preach, in a letter written to her husband after her death, says : —

"Although like most of my brethren, I felt
a strong prejudice against female preachers,
as they are termed ; and although they were
not licensed as such by our conference ; yet
my own conviction, produced by an intimate
acquaintance with her exercises of mind, was,
that if I, or any other person with whom I
was acquainted, was called of God to preach,
Sister Salome had as *great a* call, as myself. "

So severely was Sister Lincoln's mind exercised on this subject; that she was heard
to remark, that sometimes she had almost
thought, she should be willing to be lost herself, if she could be released from preaching.
But when she thought of the souls of others —
sinking down to hell, without Christ, then
she was constrained to preach.

In a letter written to Miss Liscom, she

says — * * * * * "I have given up all for Christ !—you know not the sacrifice I make in leaving my dear friends. But I wish to submit to what seems to be duty. I feel that I have sold all, for the cause in which I have engaged. I have given up earthly prospects; I have taken the parting hand of friends; — and am now going to seek a bride for my master. In another letter she says —

* * * * * "I shall soon get through with all my trials; and if faithful, it will be said to me, child! your FATHER calls, come home! and then I shall see, that I have not had one trial too many; but that they have worked out for me, a far more, and eternal weight of glory."

The strongest evidence, we can have, after all, that Sister Lincoln was called of God as a public laborer, is, the success which attended her preaching; and the deep interest which she ever felt for the salvation of others; together with the untiring zeal which she manifested in all the varied, and sometimes trying circumstances, through which she was called to pass. After she broke loose from the world, she was unceasing in her efforts. Some considerable portion of the time, she used to preach, on an average from three to four discourses a week, besides attending other meetings. And these were made the instrument in the conversion of a large number of different individuals.

Salome not only had the witness of God, and the approval of her own conscience, as an evidence of *her call;* but the hearty co-operation, of several distinguished brethren in the ministry. Her first recommendation she received from Elder Johnson, then pastor of the Reformed Methodist church at Wareham, of which she was a member. The following is a copy : —

WAREHAM, *June* 2, 1832.

" *To whom it may concern:*—This certifies that having known Sister SALOME LINCOLN for years, I am prepared to assert, that she sustains an unblemished christian character. Among her friends and neighbors she is held in *high esteem.* Having also been acquainted with the trials of her mind, in relation to her laboring publicly, I am prepared to say, she evinces a *pure sincerity* with regard to her duty. And in relation to her labors among the Reformed Methodist, they have been conducted with profit, and ability. " * * * * *

LORENZO D. JOHNSON.

Sister Lincoln, at the time she received the above, was a member of the Reformed Methodist, a denomination of respectable christians. She took a letter from the Free Will Baptists, sometime in the year 1826: and joined the class at Taunton.

About the same time, that she received the recommendation from Br. Johnson, she also received another from Br. Brett ; then Presiding Elder of the Reformed Methodist church. The following is a copy : —

" *To whom it may concern :*—This certifies, that Sister Salome Lincoln, is a person of unexceptionable character ; both moral and religious, in her own town, church, and vicinity ; and is universally approbated as a laborer in the cause of God."

PLINY BRETT.

SUCCESS AS A PREACHER. As a preacher, Sister Lincoln was very successful. She seldom preached a discourse without effect. The precise number awakened under her labors cannot be accurately ascertained. The devoted christian knows but little in this life, of the amount of good he may have accomplished. It remains to be revealed in the world of spirits ! But one thing is certain,

many were awakened and hopefully converted under her labors; and though she
received no official credentials from any body
of christians, yet most of the evangelical
denominations, were glad to receive her help.
The following recommendation which she
received from Elder Norris, — now the Editor
of the Olive Branch, * in 1834, will serve to
illustrate the manner in which her labors
were regarded.

BOSTON, *August*, 13, 1834.

" *To whom it may concern:* — As *Miss*
SALOME LINCOLN, is about to visit the State
of Maine, and is a stranger there; I would
state, that she is well known to the Christian
Public, in this section of country. She sustains a good moral character, and her con-
nections are among some of the first families
in this city, and vicinity. She is also highly
respected, as an exemplary christian. She
is approved, by a respectable, and in this
State numerous class of christians, to help
in the gospel ministry.— Many hundreds in
this city, and in the neighboring towns have

* A Paper published in Boston, Mass.

listened to her pulpit instructions, with apparent pleasure and profit. "

THOMAS F. NORRIS,
Pastor of the Reformed Methodist Church, Boston.

PREACHED HER FIRST SERMON. Sister Lincoln commenced her public labors in the vicinity of her father's, by taking part in prayer and conference meetings. Her first sermon was preached October 17th, 1827 — The meeting was held about two miles from her father's residence. She had just returned from a Quarterly Meeting, held at Rochester, Mass.; and in speaking of the meeting she says,

"I started expecting to hear Elder Brett preach. But my mind was uncommonly burdened ; and I felt that I should have something to do. As I went up to the door, a little girl met me, and informed me that the preacher had not come. The thought was immediately suggested — he will not come ! I felt almost sure of it. I went into the house, and sat down in the kitchen, while the people were assembling in another room. A large number of young persons were present, and not one among them that had ever professed religion. I sat a few moments trembling under the cross : and then fell upon my knees

and commenced praying. While in prayer,
the power of God was manifested — and the
fear of man taken away. I then arose and
began to speak. The promise of the Lord
was verified — "Open thy mouth wide, and
I will fill it." — While I spoke the eyes of
the youth were fixed upon me, and many
were affected even to tears.

After I sat down, one aged woman arose
and spoke a few words of exhortation, set-
ting forth the importance of attending to the
duties of religion while in youth. But not
feeling my mind freed, I arose again, and
spoke a few words, and then dismissed the
meeting.

I expected that much would be said in relation to this meeting; but I felt that the Lord
approbated me. And if the LORD *is for me*,
who can be against me."

STYLE OF PREACHING. Sister Lincoln's
style of preaching, by those who have heard
her, is said to have been good. In private,
as we have already noticed, she was naturally reserved and retiring in her manners.
But in the pulpit, she was bold and attracting;
and as she began to warm up in the spirit of
her discourse, this reserve was entirely gone,

In the year 1839, after her marriage, she went with her husband to the town of New-port, R. I. * — and preached in one of the largest meeting-houses in that place. Says Elder McKenzie, who was then pastor of the church — "In reference to her preach-ing at Newport, it was thought she would class with any female preacher, who had ever been there. In her discourse, there was no artificial arrangement; yet clearness of reasoning — the argument sound — and the motives warm, and from the heart. The seats were all filled, and many were forced to stand."

She usually preached without notes, and sometimes with but little premeditation. On another occasion a little girl who was accus-tomed to hear sermons read, went to hear her. After meeting, she was asked how she liked. She replied, "It was the *best sermon* I ever heard! on being asked why, she said, "because the *preacher talked out of her mouth.*"

TALENTS AS A PREACHER. For talents as a preacher, Sister Lincoln ranked above mediocrity, whether compared with male or

* Newport, a town on the Island of Rhode Island.

female. This we conclude from the fact, that she always sustained herself in that capacity, wherever she went; and frequently she preached to very large congregations; and from the testimony of individuals who are themselves men of judgment and taste. Says Eld. Joseph Whittemore, the pastor of the F. W. Baptist church at Tiverton, R. I. *
" She was the best hand in conference meetings, I ever was acquainted with. I heard her preach several times. Her discourses were talented, and delivered with spirit. " — Eld. Johnson's testimony in relation to a discourse preached at a protracted meeting in Sandwich, is to the point. It was given in a letter, written to her husband after her death. Says he : —

" Among the many scenes where I was a co-laborer and witness, in the early life of your lamented companion, there is one, which I presume, I, and many others, will never forget.

We had a protracted meeting in a grove, in the town of Sandwich, Mass. ; where we spread our tents like a camp meeting, and passed day and night on the ground.

* Tiverton is a town in the east part of the State of Rhode Island. It was formerly called Pocassett.

On the last day of the meeting, it was proposed to have a sermon at midnight. — The
lot fell upon Sister Salome to preach, and
she consented. The bright moonlight, falling
upon the thick foliage, which formed a can-
opy over our heads — produced a kind of dim
religious light, through all the arena where
we were assembled !— It being thus pleasant
and inviting — a large audience collected.—
At the appointed time, Sister Salome accompained by one or two female friends, took the
stand, and announced her text —

" And at MIDNIGHT there was a cry made ;
Behold the Bridegroom cometh ; go ye out
to meet him ! — Matt. xxv. 6.

As she entered into the subject, her heart
seemed to grow warm, her faith to increase—
and her heavy voice echoed through the
moonlight grove with rapture ! * * * * *—
Probably she never spoke with greater power,
or more effect ! — The stillness of midnight,
contrasted with the voice of warning to the
impenitent !

This sermon, I afterwards learned, was
made the power of God, unto the salvation
of several immortal souls. — One young man
who was awakened, gave himself no rest,

until he found peace in believing.   He afterwards went to sea, where he made his grave
with the monsters of the deep. — But he left
an evidence behind, that, though his body
might be rolling in the deep blue ocean, his
soul was at rest with God ! "

CHAPTER III.

MISCELLANEOUS.

"Women are not for rule designed,
Nor yet for blind submission."

HAVING in the two former chapters noticed her conversion, and some of the reasons why she supposed God had called her to preach his everlasting gospel, the reader will pardon me, if I now call his attention back to the period where we closed the first chapter.

At the time of her conversion in 1822, she was at work in the weaving room in the factory at Hopewell, Taunton, for the Richmond Company. When she commenced her labors in the factory we are unable to say; but it was probably about the year 1821. And here I would remark, that combined with piety and talent, Salome was industrious. After she began to travel and preach; as she received but little from others, she was accustomed to work with her hands to clothe herself; and then go out on her missions of

5*

love, till it was expended ; being too sensitive to say anything in relation to her circumstances, and the church too *covetous* to inquire. *
Once she was over *one hundred* miles from home, without one cent of money ; but God, who from time immemorial has supplied the wants of his children, provided friends for her, and thus she was enabled to return. The Psalmist says ;—" I have never seen the righteous forsaken, nor his seed begging bread." This is a consoling thought to the poor minister, who has sacrificed all for the cause of Christ, and embarked on the stormy sea — life's troubled ocean, perplexed with cares at home and abroad — shunned by worldly wisdom, frowned upon by the ungodly — and destined to meet with new difficulties at every corner. He that embarks in this enterprise, stimulated by hopes of gain, or self emolument, will be very liable to make shipwreck of faith before he has sailed far ! The faithful minister receives not his reward here, but in heaven.

Salome continued to work in the factory

* This remark will not apply to every place — as there were honorable exceptions—and the Lord will reward every one according to their deeds.

at Hopewell, until the first of May, 1829, when an unforeseen circumstance occurred which deprived her of work. The circumstance is briefly this :

For some cause, the corporation reduced the wages in the weaving department, where Salome was then at work. The girls indignant at this, bound themselves under an obligation, not to go back into the mill, until the former prices were restored ; and this not being granted, they formed themselves into a procession, and marched through the streets, to the green in front of the Court house. The procession started from Hopewell, about the middle of the forenoon. They were in uniform, — having on black silk dresses, with red shawls, and green calashes. They then went into a hall near the common, in order to listen to an address. Salome was selected as the orator of the day. She then took the stand, and in her own peculiar style, eloquently addressed them at considerable length, on the subject of their wrongs ; after which they quietly returned to their homes.

For one inducement, and another, nearly all who had turned out at this time, returned into the factory again, and resumed

their work. But not so with Salome!—She
manfully refused to violate her word; but
chose rather, to leave business — and break
up all the social and religious ties she had
formed; than to deviate from the paths of
rectitude. After this she never worked in
the factory again at Taunton; but sought
employment elsewhere, and was successful.

After leaving the factory at Hopewell, she
returned home, where she remained about
two weeks, and then went to Easton, Mass.
to work in the mill for Mr. Barzilla Dean. *
She worked for him at two different periods.
First from May 19th, 1829, to May 29, 1830;
when she left for a short season, but returned
in the fall of the same year, and continued
to work for him until February 4, 1831.

While living at Easton, she boarded with
her employer. Says Mr. Dean, — " When
in my family, she lived a devoted christian
life : All her leisure moments, she spent in
reading the Bible. " Says another individual ; a member of the same family : — " She
always used to kneel before retiring. It

* Mr. Dean's factory is located in Easton, about one mile
from the Meeting-house, and ten miles north of Taunton
Green.

looked strange to me then ; but it made no difference if all the girls were present ; and among her associates in the mill, there were some, who were very rude ; but she would frequently check them. "

While at Easton, she attended meeting with the Episcopal Methodist, and took a prominent part in their conferences, where her talents shone with peculiar lustre. Says Eld. Benton, who was then preaching there, " She possessed an uncommon mind for one of her sex. She was good in Scripture, and was endowed with talents, which, when consecrated to the service of God, were capable of making her extensively useful. "

In the month of June 1829, Salome was reduced very low with a fever. She was confined to her bed, at her father's in Raynham, for upwards of three weeks ; but according to her own relation her mind was stayed on God. — July 5th, although extremely weak, she was able to attend a Quarterly meeting at Rehoboth, and she gradually regained her strength, and by the blessing of God, was soon able to resume her labor.

Several years elapsed from the time Sister Lincoln preached her first sermon in 1827, until she gave herself wholly to the work ; yet she was not idle, as she improved the many opportunities that offered of doing good. During this period, she struggled on between hope and despair ; and sometimes she would leave the mill for a short season, and go out to attend meetings, and on these occasions her soul would find matter for encourage- ment, and duty would seem clear ! Had she yielded to these impressions ; undoubtedly she would have enjoyed more of the presence of God ; but individuals are not usually wil- ling to conform immediately to the convic- tions of duty, especially when it is crossing, and for this neglect God frequently severely chastises them.

In April of 1829 — Salome again attempted to preach. Whether she had preached pre- vious to this, since the time of her first dis- course, we have no notice ; but probably she did. This meeting was held at Capt. White's, in Raynham.—It was Saturday evening, and although the night was dark—and the storm fast gathering, a large number collected.— She addressed them from these words :— " Behold the Lamb of God, which taketh away the sins of the world." *St. John* i. 29.

After meeting she was requested to give out another appointment. She accordingly consented to preach the next day, (*Sunday*) at two o'clock ; but as she was going home Satan suggested to her, that she had said all that night she could, and she would have nothing remaining to add on the morrow.

The next day she went to her appointment, but without a subject. The adversary of souls, who goeth about like a roaring lion, hurled his firey darts, thick around her, and led her to believe, that if she attempted to speak, she would get confounded. The people had began to assemble, she took her Bible, but searched in vain for a text. Here she was, as Satan had told her—the hour arrived— the audience assembled—no text—no subject—and nothing to say !—What could she do ?—Perhaps she might have felt as Eld. Colby did, when on one occasion, about the first of his preaching, after getting confounded, like going to the river and drowning herself. But in this instance God who is a *present help* in every time of need, supplied her with a subject, in season to deliver a feeling discourse, from the Psalmist—"If the foundations be destroyed, what can the righteous do."—Psalms xi. 3.

She gave another appointment for the next Sabbath at a Mr. Smith's, and when the time arrived spoke from these words,—

"So the ship master came to him, and said unto him, what meanest thou *O sleeper ?* Arise and call upon thy God; if so be, God will think upon us, and we perish not !"—Jonah i. 6.

The year 1830, was noted for a powerful revival of religion in Easton, and its vicinity. It is said to have been the most extensive, ever known in that section, and in this work, Sister Lincoln was actively engaged. In speaking of it in a letter to a friend, she says : — * * * * * " The ark of the Lord seems to be moving on ! The brethren and sisters, labor like those accustomed to the yoke ! about twelve professed faith in Christ, during the first four days, and last evening we numbered about one hundred and twenty at the altar for prayers !—Since then the work has moved onward with power. This work far surpasses any thing I ever saw, all classes and ages from eleven to ninety, are the subjects of divine grace. It is still spreading with power and glory ! "

Connected with her history at Easton, are

some pleasing associations. She formed a large circle of acquaintance and friends, to whom she was ardently attached through life. Among her most intimate companions, was Sophronia Packard, who worked in the same room with her, and boarded in the same family.

Sophronia experienced religion, during the revival in Easton in 1830. She was then at home, and Salome and another lady was there on a visit, Sophronia was deeply distressed in her mind, and requested Sister Lincoln to pray with her. They then knelt together, the two ladies on either side, while Salome addressed the throne of grace in a solemn and feeling manner; and when they arose the other lady remarked to her:—

"Sophronia has received light."

"I know it—I know it !" replied Salome.

The clouds of darkness were dispelled from her mind, and the glorious Son of righteousness spoke peace to her wounded soul.

From this time, to the time of her death she lived a devoted christian. She died happy, and just before departing this life to be with Jesus, she exhorted her husband to pre-

6

pare to meet her at the judgment seat of Christ.

The day she was taken sick, seven weeks before her death, she wrote some resolutions to govern her future life ; and excepting an inscription addressed to her husband, to be placed on her tablet, this was her last business, having been taken sick the same night. The following is an extract :—

" This day do I fully surrender myself to THEE, to be thine through *Time* and ETERNITY ! All that I have, and am to be disposed of, as thou seest fit. Grant Lord to give me grace to perform, and strength to fulfil all the obligations I make this day to thee. O Lord, I beseech thee to keep me unspotted from the world ! May every morning of my life, witness a renewal of myself to thee ! * * * * * Grant me grace sufficient to keep this resolution ;—and may this solemn vow not be broken, till death seals in silence, my mortal tongue."

SOPHRONIA H. SNELL. *

She has gone ! Her happy spirit, freed from its tenement of clay, and accompained, by angels, took its flight away from earth, Sep-

* Her name after marriage.

tember 7, 1837, to reap the rich reward of the christian. She could say with the poet,—

> " Ye glittering toys of earth adieu,
> A nobler choice be mine ;
> A real prize attracts my view,
> A treasure all divine !"

Said one of old, " Let me die the death of the righteous, and let my last end be like his." There is a marked contrast between the death-bed scene of the righteous, and the ungodly, him that is prepared, and him who hath squandered life away, until his glass has run out, without securing an interest in the *kingdom of heaven !*

The ardent attachment formed between these two individuals, remained unshaken till death. The following extract from a letter, written by Sister Lincoln, will serve to show the nature of that friendship. It was written at Easton, and dated June 10, 1830.

This letter independent of the sentiment, will serve to illustrate her brilliant style of writing. I think it among one of the most excellent productions I have ever read, and would recommend it to the careful perusal of every reader. It reads as follows :—

"*Dear Friend :* — In compliance with your request, I now propose to dedicate a few lines to you, as a memorial of that friendship, which commenced with our first acquaintance, and has strengthened till I find you twining like a silver chord around my heart— A friendship so sacred that death itself cannot dessolve the tie that binds us together ! But when life's flickering lamp has ceased to burn, and our bodies are consigned to the pale mansions of the dead, I humbly trust our kindred spirits will rise through the ethereal blue, to those mansions of eternal rest, where no sorrow or distress, will ever have admittance for one moment, to mar our felicity, or disturb the aspiration of praise, to the great fountain of all happiness !

I rejoice exceedingly in the choice you have made in early life of religion. You have enlisted in the best of all causes, and some experience has taught me that wisdom's ways are ways of pleasantness, and all her paths are peace.

Though your paths may not always be strewed with thornless roses ; yet you will find by a close walk with God, every trial will be sweetened, and your path will grow brighter and brighter until the perfect day."

Yours &c.,   SALOME LINCOLN.

Life's flickering lamp in both these individuals has now gone out, and doubtless their *kindred spirits* are united in heaven ! It is a pleasing reflection to the christian, that though death may sever earthly ties ; yet in heaven we shall be re-united, forever beyond the influence of dissolution.

At the death of Sister Lincoln, the following memento was found among her papers :

TO SALOME.

" Go lovely girl o'er distant hills,
  Some friend more blest than I to find ;
And when the evening dew distills,
  Let memory call past scenes to mind !

Thy joys—thy sorrows here to share,
  Perhaps will never be my lot ;
But thou may'st grant this fervant prayer,
  Forget me not—*forget me not !*

And when the flowers of summer, bloom
  Upon the grave where I shall sleep,
Come then and on my silent tomb,
  One tear of friendship kindly weep."

                        SOPHRONIA H. PACKARD.

6*

CHAPTER IV.

THE FEMALE PREACHER.

"Go ye into all the world and preach the Gospel to every creature."—CHRIST.

> Beautiful upon the mountains,
> Are the messengers of peace."—*Adams.*

Amid all the trials, attending the labors of the faithful minister, there is a pleasure in *preaching* the *gospel*, which has its rise, from knowing that we are useful as the servants of Christ, and from complying with the conviction which God has implanted in our bosom, that it is our duty. Now if it be true, that man cannot satisfy the requisitions thus made, and hence enjoy happiness ; and if God has implanted the same conviction of duty, in the breast of woman, how can she any more than man, rest satisfied or expect happiness, unless she obey the calls of God ?

I expect that in heaven, woman will occupy as high a rank among the happy myriads, as man, and will tune her voice in the praises

of God, as high as any of the angels, who
have sung in paradise for ages. But her
voice will be melodious there, in proportion
to her faithfulness here. This being the case
there is an incentive for *woman*, as well as
man, to *forsake* all and *follow* CHRIST.

It was this that actuated Salome to leave
father and mother, brother and sister, neighbors and friends, and to break up all the
social relations of life in order to *Preach the
Gospel ;* and if there is joy in heaven over
one sinner that repenteth, who would wish to
deprive her, or any other woman from par-
ticipating in that joy.

As the spring of 1830 wore away, and as
the tender buds began to swell, and summer's
splendor to dawn, her heart expanded with
benevolence ; and she began to feel still more
deeply for the lost condition of a dying world.
In view of this she resolved to forsake all,
and proclaim the glad tidings of salvation.
Accordingly May 18th, she left the factory at
Easton, and made preparation for more ex-
tended usefulness.

One week before she left Easton, as she
was returning on the Sabbath from meeting,
she stopped by the way at *five o'clock* to at-

tend a conference. A cloud of darkness, according to her own relation, hovered over her mind, and she felt as though her soul was barren, and she should have nothing to do or say. She entered the room, and took her seat, but on casting her eye around, discovered one with whom she labored.

This girl was seriously inclined, and one whom Salome highly esteemed; but of anything further, she was not aware. Yet there was a silent whispering within, which told her that all was not right. As the contest was going on between the enemy and the spirit, Salome arose to speak; and the first word she uttered was like a nail, fastened in a sure place; it sunk deep into the heart of her friend, and when the meeting closed, she found her under deep concern of mind for the salvation of her soul. From this meeting they repaired to a class meeting, where her friend was soon *basking* in the sunshine of God's *Eternal Love*, his spirit testifying with her spirit, that she was born again.

The first discourse that Sister Lincoln preached after leaving Easton, was at Hopewell, at the residence of Mrs. Hall. It being the place where she had formerly worked,

and many of her old acquaintance still remaining, she naturally had fears in relation
to what they would think and say. But notwithstanding this she went boldly forward in
the discharge of duty, and when the hour for
meeting arrived, the house was crowded with
spectators, many of whom had doubtless
come with no other view, than to hear *Salome
Lincoln.* There are many individuals, who
will turn out to meeting when some stranger,
or exciting preacher is to be present, when
in the same places, on ordinary occasions,
the house of God is left desolate.

Her text on this occasion, was from Deu.
xxxii. 11, 12, " As an eagle stirreth up her
nest, fluttereth over her young, spreadeth
abroad her wings, taketh them, beareth them
on her wings ; so the *Lord alone did lead him,*
and there was no *strange god* with him. "

This sermon was preached the 28th of
May, and the next day being Saturday, she
went in company with Miss Liscom * to a
town a few miles S. W. of Taunton, where

* Elizabeth Liscom, now French. To her Salome was
ardently attached, and from her she received as much en-
couragement during her severe trials, as from any other individual.

she spent the Sabbath. During the day she attended meeting with the ———, * and listened to the discourse of a young man by the name of B * * * *. At six o'clock that evening, being requested, she consented to preach in a school house, in the immediate vicinity ; but during the interval strong opposition was raised among some of the brethren, and when arrived at the place of appointment, they found that no preparation had been made, and the door fast locked. However, two ladies went and obtained the key, and opened the door. The house was soon *densely crowded*, and as not near all could get in, they were forced to take out the windows, in order that those outside might hear. She commenced the exercises by giving out the following hymn, well adapted, not only to her own feelings, but to the occasion.—

> "Savior of men, thy searching eye,
> Doth all my inmost thoughts descry ;
> Doth aught on earth, my wishes raise
> Or the world's pleasure, or its praise ?

* The name of the town, together with the denomination and individuals, are kept behind the curtain, as strong sectarian prejudice was probably manifested, and the respect we have to individual feeling, leads us not to name them.

The love of Christ, doth me constrain,
  To seek the *wandering souls of men;*
With cries, entreaties, tears to save,
  To snatch them from the gaping grave.

For this let men *revile my name ;*
  No cross I shun, I fear no shame :
All hail *reproach !* and welcome pain—
  Only *thy terrors,* Lord restrain !

Give me thy strength, O God of power!
  Then let winds blow, and thunders roar;
Thy *faithful witness* will I be,
  Tis fixed — *I can do all through* THEE !"

No one can tell the conflicting emotions, which filled the breast of Salome on this occasion. The embarrassing circumstances under which she was placed, was enough to have put to test the feelings of the harder sex.

Urgently requested to preach, by those too, whom she reasonably presumed were her friends, and then as she moved forward, innocently, and honestly, as she thought in the discharge of duty—to find herself alone, and unprotected save by a few female friends, the way apparently hedged up, the door locked against her, and to witness the silent whisperings of scornful reproach, was extremely severe. But in justice to our departed Sister, and others concerned, we are bound to say ; that if there was any prejudice previously existing, it was of but short duration, as on the next day, she received through the hands of Miss Liscom, the following polite note :—

" *Sister Lincoln :*—Without doubt you have heard that I did not like to have you preach in this neighborhood. That report is not true, for I should be glad to have you preach here often. The report was through misunderstanding, or evil intentions. The reason why I did not attend meeting, was, my business rendered it impracticable. I should be glad to have you come and preach here, whenever you can make it convenient. And when our house is finished, our pulpit shall be at your service."

Yours with Christian affection,

***** *****

She remained at * * * * about two weeks, and held other meetings, and then returned to Taunton.

She next went to Rochester Neck. Rochester is a town in the southern part of Plymouth county. At Rochester she found many friends, among whom were Eldrs. Johnston and Minor, and while here she preached several times; once in a school house on Rochester Neck. The notice had been previously given out by Eld. Johnston, — the house was well filled, and the Lord manifested his presence in the midst. She says:—"I felt rather awkward on account of Elder Johnston being present, but I made the best of it I could, and as soon as I had concluded, he gave out notice that I would preach again in the evening. I went to my appointment that evening, as deliberately as ever I went to a day's work in my life. The house was very much crowded, besides a large number who could not get in, and were forced to stand outside."

The next Sabbath she attended a meeting, and preached in the same neighborhood; but so large a number assembled at the school house, that it was thought best to hold the meeting in a grove near by. Elder Johnston preached in the morning, and Sister Lincoln in the afternoon. The scene on this occasion was truly sublime. Surrounded as she was by a large concourse of people, of both sexes, and of all ages, some of whom had come miles to hear *The Female Preacher*, and

7

who then stood listening with breathless attention to the plain truths of the gospel, as they eloquently escaped from her lips, while she stood sheltered from the scorching rays of the sun, under the spreading branches of a lofty tree. The next Sabbath after, she preached in what is called the *Old Spruce* Meeting-house in Middleborough. * With regard to her discourse there, but little is known by the author. She spent several weeks in preaching in this section, and then left for the Cape. After leaving Rochester she spent several months in preaching at Harwich, Chatham, Orleans, Falmouth and Brewster. At Brewster she was the happy witness of several hopeful conversions.

She went to Falmouth sometime in the month of September, to a camp-meeting held at a place commonly called Wayquoit, and sometimes East Falmouth. On the fourth day of the meetings the preachers were obliged to leave, but Salome remained. The work of the Lord already powerfully begun, was

* Middleborough is in the South West part of Plymouth County; and the Old Spruce meeting-house, now standing, is about six miles South East from Middleborough Four Corners.

rapidly spreading, and twelve individuals who
on the morning of that day were in the gall
of bitterness and in the bonds of iniquity,
before night were rejoicing in the Lord.

She continued to hold meetings for the
several succeeding nights, and a large number more were converted. In speaking of
this revival, she says, — "The Lord has
worked like himself—a wonder working God.
It is the Lord's doings, and it is marvellous
in our eyes. It cannot be said in this neighborhood, as it is frequently said in others,
during revivals of religion, that it is only
among the weak and silly women, or the
lower classes in society, for it is chiefly confined to the young men, and those too of
promising talents, and from the first class in
society."

And here I would add ; how frequently is
the ear pained, and the heart of the faithful
christian melted by expressions like those
alluded to in the above, and that too from
men, whose convictions of truth and duty, at
the same time, teach them better — just as
though HEAVEN and *Immortal Glory*, was
good enough for the POOR and *despised !—*
But as for them, they have no concern about

the *future!* Such men, will do well to reflect, that they have a soul to be saved or lost,
a *soul* of *immortal* worth !—Yes, *ten thousand
worlds* like this, with all its riches, and honors would not pay for the *Ransom* of such a
soul ! And again they will do well to reflect
upon the death-bed scene of Thomas Paine,
and some other noted infidels ; who, as the
lamp of life went out were left in the most
abject misery, calling upon an *insulted* SAVIOR
to *have mercy !*

It was during this revival, that two young
men, Benjamin and Simeon Eldrich were
converted. They were men of promising
talent, highly respected among their acquaintance, and devotedly pious. What is still
more remarkable, but a short time after their
conversion, they had strong presentiment of
their approaching death. They both followed
the sea, and Simeon but a few days before
he left home for the last time, went through
the neighborhood—took leave of the hills
and trees, and as he left each family, invari-
ably remarked, that it was his fixed conviction that he should never return. About the
same period he attended a meeting in the
vicinity, and there remarked,— " Some doubt

that I am willing to die.   They say, it is faith
untried!   I will think of it, I am willing to
die!—I will think of it again — *I am willing
to die!* — I will think of it thrice — I AM WIL-
LING TO DIE!—The moment my spirit leaves
the body, it will be in *immortal glory!* " —
Who after witnessing such christian fortitude,
can for a moment doubt the virtue of religion,
or, that

> " Jesus can make a dying bed,
> Feel soft as downy pillows are. "

Soon after this, he went to sea in a vessel
bound for New York, and was lost!

Benjamin, though equally impressed with
a conviction that the hour drew near for him
to depart this life, yet being more retiring,
said less about it, to those around him. He
was lost from the Schooner Spy, bound from
New York to Baltimore. He was passing
the lead in the evening, in order to get the
sounding, and unperceived fell overboard,
and was drowned. They have gone from
whence no traveller returns; but in the language of the sacred penman,—" Blessed are
the dead that die in the Lord."

Sister Lincoln remained at East Falmouth,
and vicinity, until about the last of October.

7*

Her time while there was well spent, in preaching, visiting and attending conferences. From a letter written home to her parents, we learn that while gone, at this time, she preached between thirty and forty discourses. This for a female just beginning, and not in the enjoyment of very good health was a large amount of labor.

An anecdote is related of her while on the Cape in 1830 showing her ardent attachment to the cause of Christ, and the deep interest she felt in the salvation of others. A party was collected to go to the beach to enjoy a short recreation, and among those who joined them, were two young men, who I should judge had not much respect for themselves, for religion, or for any thing else of a weighty character. They were seated on what is called by those who reside on the beach a Horsefoot. Salome in her usually friendly and feeling manner, went up to them and enquired if they enjoyed religion. The only reply they made was, this Horsefoot is —————— hard, and rudely left her. But if their consciences were not seared as with a hot iron, they heard those words resounding in their ears for more than one twenty-four hours after, and if now living out of Christ, though her tongue is silenced in death, yet she speaketh in an audible voice, in the language then used—"YOUNG MEN! *do you enjoy religion ?*" Prepare before your day of probation ceases, to answer this question, at the judgment seat of Christ !

After returning home, she went back to work in the factory at Easton, where she remained till sometime in the month of February 1831, when she bid a final adieu to the factories, for a higher and nobler calling.

> " How beauteous are their feet,
> Who stand on *Zion's Hill ;*
> Who bring *salvation* on their tongues,
> And words of peace reveal ! "

With these passing remarks on the life of Sister Lincoln, I shall now close the chapter; and in doing which, it is becoming that we pause and reflect. In the life of Sister Lincoln, we see exemplified in a striking manner, not only a strong mind, a resolute perseverence—a character signalized for its deep toned piety, and strict adherence to truth ; but the sacred regard of God for his children.

CHAPTER V.

THE FEMALE PREACHER.

Continued.

"Home, thy joys are passing lovely;
Joys no stranger heart can tell,
Happy home, indeed I love thee —
Can I, can I say *farewell?* "

ONLY those who have been called away from the endearments of home, can conceive of the feelings that agitate the bosom, as the hour rapidly hastens on, when we are to separate ourselves from those we love, and leave the scenes of youth behind, for a residence among strangers. It is then that the past with all its beauties, and the future with all its forbodings, crowd in upon the mind, mingling pain with pleasure. In youth, time lays her finger heavily upon *memory*, and stamps her images with indelible impress; so that on an occasion like the one I am describing, we remember all the pleasing associations connected with youth.

It is then, that we call to mind the many happy hours we have spent under the fostering care of our parents—We remember the sports of childhood—Our school-day scenes— and how, that let loose from confinement, our hearts would bound with joy, and our bodies glad to be freed, would keep time to its action, as we sped away to join our merry companions. And as we sat at the window of the coach, which was bearing us away, gazing upon objects rendered familiar from having been oft visited, we realized, perhaps for the first time, how far short earthly pleasures fall of imparting happiness! And then too we felt the uncertainty of life.

Perhaps this is the last—came to the mind with force, and stole a tear! I have stood around the bed of a dear earthly relative, * and heard the last expiring breath, as the spirit took its departure, and seen the eye silently close in death, and felt to say, "thy will be done." I felt on such an occasion that my loss was his eternal gain. But to tear myself from home, knowing not where my lot might be cast, or how my path might be strewed—and called to gaze upon the faces of those I loved, knowing not where we should meet again, far surpassed every

* A Father.

thing else, I have ever experienced. Many
a time on such an occasion, I have felt to say
with the poet,

> Can I — can I say *farewell?*

But after a few more such meetings and
partings, have come and gone, we shall ALL
part or *meet*, to part no more !

Sometime in the month of May or June 1831,
Sister Lincoln again left home, to spend the
summer in Barnstable and Dukes Co's., Mass.
Previous to this date she had spent but little
time out of her own immediate circle of
acquaintance, except for a short season to
visit or preach. But now the scale turned ;
as after the spring of 1831, she only occasionally visited home — and from 1831 to the
time of her marriage, she was constantly im-
merging into new society, and forming new
associations.

The first place she visited, after leaving
home this summer, (1831) was Pocassett, a village in Sandwich, * Mass. She went to Po-
casset to attend a protracted meeting, and
while there stopped in the family of Br. Alvin
Swift. She preached several times, and from

* A town in the North West part of Barnstable County.

there went again to East Falmouth, the place
where she visited and preached in 1830.

Her labors here, were in conjunction with
those of a young man by the name of Pierce,
a preacher among the Reformed Methodist.
He had been preaching there for some time,
and was successful in winning souls to Christ.
At this time Salome preached for several
weeks, and occasionally visited there for one
or two of the following years. And besides
the places which we shall mention, there are
probably a large number of others, in the
vicinity and adjoining towns, where she visited, of which we have no definite knowledge.

It is not my object to trace her in all her
journeyings from town to town, and village
to village, and give a minute description of
every place and sermon, and in fact it would
be impossible; and such a course would
prove both monotonous and uninteresting.
Therefore if I lay before the reader, some of
the more prominent details, I shall have accomplished all he can reasonably expect.

From East Falmouth she went to Holmes'
Hole, a village which takes its name from its
harbor, in the town of Tisbury, on Martha's
Vineyard. Martha's Vineyard embraces one

entire county, (Duke's,) and is situated in
the South East part of Mass. It is an island,
about six miles from the main land. Holmes'
Hole is on the north side. It has a beautiful harbor, which makes a safe resort for
vessels during a storm. Martha's Vineyard,*
like Nantucket is *isolated* from the rest of the
world ; and one would almost suppose that
its inhabitants, could enjoy the *paradise* of
Eden.

Besides the one already named, (Tisbury)
there are two other large towns, Chilmark
and Edgartown ; at these places Salome spent
considerable time.

She went to Martha's Vineyard about the
first of July 1831, † with Bro. Hiram Chase
and wife. Bro. Chase was at East Falmouth
on a visit, where he spent the Sabbath, with
his wife's mother. Salome had for a long

---

* Martha's Vineyard, Nantucket, and I think the Elizabeth Islands, as related by tradition, derived their names
from the three daughters of a wealthy gentleman, Martha,
Nancy, and Elizabeth, who received those lands as their
possession. For the truth of this I shall not be responsible.

† Sister Chase states, that they carried her to the island for the first time she was ever there, in 1831. She
s probably correct ; but I find one reference, and only one
of her being there in 1830, which is probably incorrect.

time wished to visit the island; but till now, the way never seemed to be open.

On the Sabbath alluded to, Br. Pierce preached in the forenoon, and Salome in the afternoon. She had for several days been unwell, and that day so much so, that she kept her bed until the time of meeting, and then went to her appointment.

After meeting Mrs. Chase proposed that she should accompany them to the Vineyard, remarking at the same time, that she might make it her home with them, as long as she remained on the island.* Having had strong impressions that God had something for her to do there, she cheerfully accepted the kind offer, and accordingly made immediate preparation to leave East Falmouth.

The first place she preached on the Vineyard, was at the old meeting-house belonging to the Calvinist Baptist in Holmes' Hole. Her text was:—"Is there no *balm in Gilead?* is there no PHYSICIAN *there?—Jeremiah* viii. 22.

On this occasion she spoke to a crowded house, and a listening congregation; and many who heard her, were *melted to tears.*

After this she frequently preached there,

* Br Chase's residence is at Holmes' Hole.

8

but not much in the meeting-houses, as the
desks were made the *sanctum sanctorum,* and
were too sacred for the proclamation of *Free*
and *unmerited Salvation,* from the lips of one
of God's Female Servants.*   But we have
reason to rejoice that the Gospel is the power
of God unto salvation, whether it is preached
by a D. D., or a common *Street Beggar.*—
And still more, it is declared :—" God hath
chosen the FOOLISH THINGS of the world, to
confound the *Wise ;* and God hath chosen
the *Weak Things* of the world, *to confound
the things* which are MIGHTY." †   While she
remained at Holmes' Hole, she held her
meetings principally at private houses ;   and
by a strict christian deportment, she gathered
many worthy friends around her, many of
whom, will remember her labors there with
gratitude and thanksgiving to God.

Says a friend : — " I expect to see her in a

* It is worthy of note, that after spending much time in
another section of the Island, and witnessing many hopeful conversions, and after gathering around her a large circle
of christian friends, who were attached to her, and that
when about leaving, she remarked to a friend, " I have no
pastor to send them, and Br. B——— must take charge of
the LAMBS of the *flock.*

† 1 Cor. i. 27.

few days.* Salome will stand in her *lot* and
place! Her preaching here was powerful.
The *aged*, the middle-aged and young, of
both sexes, and from all ranks in society,
were awakened and led to seek an interest
in Christ."

On the 25th of July she left Holmes' Hole,
and went to North Shore, another part of
Tisbury, about four miles from the last named
place. The circumstances connected with
her going to North Shore, are briefly these:
Having heard of her preaching at Holmes'
Hole, several individuals from there, came
down to attend the meetings ; and after
meeting, being urgently requested to visit
that place, she consented to go. In view of
going there, she remarked to a friend :—

" It is GOD that *calls*, and *I must go!* "

The remaining part of the year 1831, and
a portion of 1832 and '33, she spent in preaching, and holding meetings at the North Shore
and in the adjoining section. The Lord was
with her, and witnessed her labors, by giving
her souls, as seals of her ministry. There is
nothing more encouraging to the christian

* The individual alluded to here, is a firm, though con-
scientious believer in the second advent of Christ, in 1843.

minister, than to see the sinner turning from the error of his ways, and becoming a devoted christian — beloved in the church, and useful in the world! The sacred penman says : — " Let him know, that he which converteth a sinner from the error of his ways, shall save a soul from death, and hide a multitude of sins."—James v. 20.

While at the North Shore, she generally preached at the school-house, but sometimes at a grove near by, in order to accommodate the large number who came to hear.

The grove is a delightful spot, fitted up with seats, for the purpose of holding meetings during the summer months. On one occasion, while preaching at this place, in speaking of the tree under which she then stood, she said, — " When my body *sleeps in the dust*, this tree will speak." This remark is now distinctly remembered by those who then heard her, and in 1842, nine years afterwards, when a meeting of a similar character was again to be held there, they were particular in selecting the same tree for the preachers' stand ; and the fact of her having preached there, was several times mentioned. How pleasant a spot is often rendered for having been the *resort* of departed friends.

On another occasion, (Sabbath morning,) as she came down from her chamber, she was in tears on account of her trials of mind. But she preached all day at the grove ; in the forenoon from a passage in the *twenty-fifth* chapter of Matthew, and in the afternoon from Acts xxvi. 13 — " At mid-day, O king ! I saw in the way, a light from heaven, *above the brightness of the Sun.*" Says the individual who related this circumstance — " I seldom ever listened to a discourse, with so profound attention as on this occasion. I should not hesitate in pronouncing it, EVANGELICAL, *beautiful* and sublime !" *

The same individual heard her preach again, a short time after, from a text in Isaiah.

The arrangement of her discourses, was usually very clear, and her divisions distinctly marked, but as they were mental rather than written, we have not been able to give much in relation to the matter. But in this

---

* This was related by Mr. Anthony Luce, a gentleman who is blind : and individuals of this class, usually hear more critically, than those who are blessed with perfect organs.

8*

instance Mr. Luce gave us what he thinks a correct skeleton; and as we have not heretofore, and shall not probably hereafter be able to give a specimen, we will now insert it.

"And a HIGHWAY shall be there, and a way, and it shall be called, *The way of holiness.*"—Isaiah xxxv. 8.

She divided the subject in the following manner: viz.—

I. SHE SPOKE OF THE HIGHWAY.
Christ is the great *Highway.*

II. SHE CONSIDERED THE WAY TO THE HIGHWAY.

We are led to the Highway,
(1.) By *Consideration.*
(2.) By *Prayer.*
(3.) By *Faith.*
(4.) By *Repentance.*
(5.) By living HOLY LIVES, &c.

The following is an extract of a letter written to Elizabeth Liscom, and will show more fully the success attending her preaching this summer. It was written at

TISBURY, *September 5th,* 1831.

"*Dear Eliza:*—* * * * * After camp-meeting I spent three weeks in East Falmouth,

and from there I came to the Vineyard, but
did not expect to stop more than one or two
weeks. At the first meeting I had in this
place, I felt an uncommon anxiety for the
people, yet I left the neighborhood, after
spending one Sabbath. * * * * * * I then
went to the harbor,* which is about four
miles, but the people followed me in my im-
agination, and I had no rest, till a few days
after, when a man came for me to go back.
* * * * * At the first meeting I held after returning, one backslider was reclaimed, and
I have thought every week since, that I should
leave the next, but the time has never come
when I dared to go. I have now been here
two months, and there is a greater prospect
of my staying than ever. The cloud which I
saw the first day I was here, has been increasing ever since, and a number of backsliders have been reclaimed, one soul converted, and several more anxiously inquiring
to know what they shall do to be saved.
I have been called to converse with one, who
was so deeply distressed that she was obliged
to leave her school to come and see me ; and
though she went away as she came, yet I

* Holmes' Hole.

believe that she is near the kingdom of heaven.
I have had some pretty severe trials since I
have been here, yet· no more than has been
for my good. * * * * * I shall wait with impa-
tience to hear from you.

Yours as ever,

SALOME LINCOLN."

The young lady referred to in the above
letter, was probably Emily Look, now the
wife of Mr. Leonard Luce. She was the
first individual that was converted at the
North Shore, under Sister Lincoln's preaching. The meeting where she was awakened
was held at Mr. Edmund Luce's, sometime
in the month of September, 1831.* While
Sister Salome was speaking, her mind was
so powerfully impressed, that she lost her
self-control, and fell from her seat. Sister
Lincoln stopped preaching, and went to her,
and commenced praying. She exhorted her
to say : —

> " Here Lord I give myself away,
> 'Tis all that I can do."

The next evening, (Saturday,) another
meeting was held at the residence of Br. David

---

* It might have been in 1830, though Sister Luce thinks
it was in 1831.

Butler. Miss Look was still in great distress, but before the meeting closed, her burden left her, and soon she was singing praises and thanksgiving to him who had delivered her soul from the gall of bitterness and the bonds of iniquity.

Sister Luce is still living in the enjoyment of religion ; and among all the converts awakened under her preaching, none seemed to produce a deeper effect upon the mind of Salome, as may be seen from a letter written by her ; the following is an extract ; *

RAYNHAM, *May* 15*th*, 1831.

" *Dear Sister Emily :*—It was with pleasure that I received your letter. 'I was glad to hear that you were trying to serve the Lord. O Sister, I feel a deep interest in your prosperity ! You was the first I saw converted while I was on the Vineyard ; and although young, may you be a pattern of piety to those around you, and while others may treat the subject with indifference, may it not dis-

---

* This letter has evidently been read and re-read, till it was literally worn up, so much so that it could never have had a place in this memoir, had not the author took a copy, as Sister Luce read a part, and from memory, having almost committed it, rehearsed the rest.

courage you in your path to heaven. Emily, be determined to be a christian in every sense of the word! Pray and watch over your deportment ; and in order for this, let me advise you to spend a short season in prayer every morning. This will prepare you for the employments of the day, and will enable you to enter upon them with a suitable frame of mind. Be determined to do nothing that you cannot feel that God approves ; and never fear to be singular, when the customs of those around you are in opposition to the spirit of religion, but let the world know that you are determined to be the Lord's.— And may he bless you abundantly, and give you strength to resist every temptation, for I am sensible you will have many. Dear Emily, my heart almost bleeds, when I think of your youth, and the trials to which you will be exposed, especially while the profes- sors of the religion of Jesus are in a luke- warm state. Should you backslide, and wound the innocent cause of the *Dear Redeemer*, it would rend my poor heart. Yes, I should much rather hear that you had gone to your long home in the triumphs of faith, than that you had renounced your belief in Christ.

But I will hope better things. I trust that
should I ever be permitted to come that way
again, I shall find you growing in grace, and
in the *knowledge of the truth* as it is in *Christ
Jesus;* and should we never be permitted to
meet on earth, may we meet, where parting
will be known no more ! * * * * * I hardly
know where to close, for when I get to think-
ing about the Vineyard people, I think of
so many that I want to see, and so much
that I want to say, that I hardly know where
to stop. But I must close.

Yours, affectionately,

SALOME LINCOLN."

Soon after the conversion of Emily Look
another individual — an intelligent young man
was awakened ; it was at an evening meeting,
held in the school house. He had just returned from sea, and went to hear her, and
after sermon, Sister Lincoln gave an invitation for those who desired special prayers,
to arise. He arose, remarking at the same
time, that he did not do it from any particular impression, but from a settled conviction
of duty. It would be better, I apprehend,
for the christian community, if every one
acted from this principle. If this were the

case, the church would have less occasion to mourn over backsliders. He afterwards professed a hope in Christ, and is now a worthy member of *His visible Church.*

Another fact is worthy of notice. While at the North Shore, she formed a Female Enquiring Meeting. These meetings have been continued until the present time, and have resulted in good.

Her labors were not confined to the North Shore, nor exclusively to any particular denomination. She was not possessed with narrow contracted sectarian views, it was not congenial with her nature. Whenever, or wherever she found the image of Christ, soul mingled with soul, and to such a one, she felt that she was bound by a chord stronger than earthly, and by ties dearer than those which unite parties, sects and denominations; and with such a one, though she might differ on some minor points, she could heartily join, in carrying forward all the benevolent enterprises of the day. Hers was a Divine mission; her *credentials* she received from the Prince of princes, and to his tribunal alone she stood accountable. Those who are so happy as to get to heaven, will find but one sect, one sentiment, and one feeling. There we shall all be united in enhancing the bliss of paradise.

As opportunity offered while on the Vineyard, she went out into other places, and before the close of the year, she had been nearly over the island; and on several occasions received flattering invitations to preach in societies of a different denomination from the one to which she belonged. The following will serve as a specimen :

TISBURY, *September* 3*d*, 1831.

The undersigned, being a committee, legally authorized to supply the pulpit in the *Congregationalist Meeting-house*, of Tisbury with a Teacher, would be very glad to hear *Miss Lincoln* preach next *Sabbath*, or any other convenient time.

We are very respectfully yours.

C. G. A———

M. M———

Among other places where she preached on the Vineyard, was Edgarton and Chilmark.* She preached at Edgarton sometime

---

* In relation to her labors at Chilmark, we know nothing definite, more than that she preached there at the residence of a Mr. Luce. We find notice of her being at Edgarton several different periods.

between the first and middle of December;
but nothing more, than that she was counte-
nanced by the collector of the port, can be
accurately stated, as to the success which
attended her visits, but we may reasonably
suppose that heaven smiled on her untiring
exertions for the salvation of immortal souls
here, as well as in other places. The air she
breathed on this secluded spot was wafted
from the atmosphere of heaven. It was un-
tainted by party corruption, and unimpreg-
nated by the damp vapors of the lower regions.

Party feelings, and the divisions in the
church, have done more to promote INFIDEL-
ITY than all the combined efforts of Hume,
Paine, Voltaire, and a host of others. There
will be no *jarring* or *party strife* in HEAVEN,
but in the language of Dr. Dwight :—" The
happiness of heaven is not only unmingled,
and consummate ; not only *uninterrupted* and
immortal ; but *ever progressive.*"

Salome has gone to the haven of eternal rest, where many of the ransomed, not
only from Martha's Vineyard, but elsewhere,
will soon join her. She stands at the portal
of heaven, ready to hail their happy spirits,

as freed from the *clogs of earth,* one by one, they take their flight away to the blessed mansions of the Saints.

With the close of this year (1831) Salome left the Vineyard, and returned to East Falmouth, and from thence to Raynham, to visit her friends.

Martha's Vineyard is separated from the main land by the Vineyard sound;* and all communication to and from, is carried on with boats. The mail is transported in a ferry-boat which runs from Falmouth to Holmes' Hole. It sometimes happens, that though the sea is perfectly calm in the harbor, yet before you have fairly made out from land, you find yourself tossed about in the midst of rough water.

It was in this boat that Salome crossed when she left the Vineyard. When they started from the wharf, Mr. Ray the ferry-man, observed, that he had not had so good a prospect of a pleasant voyage for more than two months. Besides Salome, there was one other passenger. They had not proceeded far, however, before the prospect entirely

* The distance across the sound, from Falmouth to Holmes' Hole is about six miles.

changed—the wind commenced blowing severely—the sea was boisterous, and the prospect any thing but encouraging. The waves
dashed so high, and beat against the boat
with such violence, that they found it exceedingly difficult to keep their seats. They arrived
at Falmouth about sunset, having been tossed
about on the briny deep for the most part of
the afternoon. She says, " I expected to have
had to remain at Falmouth until the next
morning, but as good fortune would have it,
five minutes after I landed, Bro. Kimball, from
East Falmouth with a horse and sleigh, called
for me, and carried me directly there."

Thus closed her labors for the year 1831;
and in closing this chapter, I remark, that
but few individuals have been more incessant
in their exertion to do good, that Sister Salome. And though oftentimes wearied with
the monotonous round of duty, and oftentimes severely tried, yet she could respond
with the poet—

> " There is a home of peaceful rest,
>   To mourning wanderers given ;
> There is a tear for souls distressed,
>   A balm for every wounded breast—
> Tis found alone—in HEAVEN !"

Besides preaching a large number of sermons, and attending other meetings, she also
labored with her hands, in order to supply
herself with the necessary articles of apparel,
and to meet the incidentary expenses attending her travels, and in every way strove to be
useful in the cause of Christ by winning souls
to him.

CHAPTER VI.

THE FEMALE PREACHER.

Concluded.

"Whosoever doth not bear his cross, and come after me, cannot be my disciple."—*Christ.*

Scenes of love and sacred friendship,
I will bid you all farewell;
O'er the earth's wide face to wander,
News of Jesus' love to tell!

In this life, we anticipate much happiness from the future, and eagerly grasp at objects not yet attained, and ere we reach them, they have like the empty bubble, quickly vanished away—the main happiness being derived from anticipation.

Reader is not this strictly true?

How many sleepless nights you have spent in meditating upon some scene of pleasure, which you fondly anticipated would yield a full cup of happiness; but alas! when the day and the hour arrived, how often has some trivial event, frustrated all your plans, and sent you away sadly disappointed!

"But why is it so?" you ask.

In reply, I would answer, it arises from the *unstable nature* of all earthly objects, and their insufficiency, without the aid of a *higher* and *nobler principle*, of imparting true happiness.

Moses understood this, when he chose to suffer affliction with the *people of God*, preferring the reproach of Christ, to the treasures of Egypt.*

The three *Pious Jews*, understood this, when they chose to obey the *King of* KINGS, and suffer the *scorching flames* of a FIERY FURNACE, *seven times heated*, rather than to bow down to a wicked monarch.†

Daniel understood this, when he chose a *den of Lions*, to the honors of the Medo-Persian Empire, and to serve the God of heaven, rather than his impious king.‡

The Prophets understood this, as the peaceably yielded their lives between the *temple* and *altar*,§ rather than to conform to the wicked customs of their backslidden nation.

Stephen understood this, when he sweetly

---

* Heb xi. 24, 25.

† Daniel iii. Chapter.

‡ Daniel vi. 1–24.

§ Acts vii. 52. Matthew xxiii. 34–36.

breathed out his life, in the midst of his per-
secutors, rather than cease to testify of Christ
and him crucified.*

All the martyrs, primitive christians, and
the true church, understand, that in order to
become a disciple of Jesus Christ, and meet
with *Divine Favor*, and enjoy solid, unfading
happiness, they must bid farewell to all the
sinful pleasures of the world—be willing to
bear his cross, and to have their names cast
out as evil; and if necessary to go to the
stake—the scaffold—to the *burning flames*,
and in a word, to suffer martyrdom in all its
varied forms, rather than sacrifice TRUTH on
the altar of *error*. Here is the basis of true
happiness—it is a *choice pearl* of great price,
and is found alone in *religion*. He that seeks
to find it in the world, will seek in vain.

Our beloved Sister, whose memoir we are
transmitting, understood this, when she at last
yielded to duty, (though she knew it would
make her unpopular,) and began publicly to
testify of Christ, and him crucified.

But I am digressing, and to return:—On
the first of January 1832, we find Salome
again visiting at Raynham; but by the fourth

* Acts vii. 54–60.

of February, she was mingling her prayers, with the prayers of her friends on Martha's Vineyard.

The year 1832, is one that will long be remembered in this country, on account of the cholera, which to some extent raged, spreading terror through the land. However, it was not so severely felt in New England, as was generally feared.

When Sister Lincoln arrived at Holmes' Hole, a ship from Europe was lying there, on board of which, two individuals had died of this dreadful malady, and in consequence of this, as might be expected, much excitement prevailed over the island. In life, we are in the midst of death; but so long as we enjoy health and its attendant blessings, we have but few fears. The sailor in calm weather, may vainly boast of his daring exploits, and tell how he can brave the dangers of the deep; but let the scene suddenly change, let clouds gather—the winds arise—the tempest increase, and the waves roll mountains high, tossing his frail bark about with unmanageable fury, threatening to engulph him in immediate destruction; and you no longer hear him tell of his courage and skill, but his cry is, "*What shall I do to be saved?*" And this feeling is not peculiar alone to the sailor, but it is witnessed in all the varied walks of life. Let danger approach, and let the last earthly refuge be taken from us, and whatever may have been our former principles, we seek protection alone in God.

About the *eighteenth* of March, (1832,) Sister Lincoln was the happy witness of another hopeful conversion to God. The subject of Divine favor in this instance, was, Mary C. Cottell, wife of Capt. Charles Cottell, at the *North Shore.* She relates the circumstance as follows:—"When I first heard this child of God, in 1832, I was in a state of sin and unbelief; but as she set forth the love of God to man—the beauties of His *holy religion*—and His readiness to save unto the uttermost all who came unto him, I felt that I was a lost sinner, and destitute of a hope in Christ. But by Sister Lincoln, I was led to the Savior as my only hope, and through her instrumentality, and the blessing of God, I was converted. Often has her supplicating voice been raised for me, and not for me only, but for many others, who were led to embrace the Savior, through her preaching."

Many more such witnesses might be gathered had we time, and means to devote to it, but were we to multiply them here, it would add but little interest to this work ; and it is my aim to avoid repetition as far as practicable, but in a work of this character it is impossible entirely to do so.

From a letter dated April 18, 1832, we learn that Sister Lincoln was at Edgarton, Martha's Vineyard, waiting for an opportunity to go to Nantucket.

Nantucket is an island *ten miles* east of Martha's Vineyard, and *twenty-four* south of Cape Cod. It is a place of considerable business, and in 1840 contained 9,512 inhabitants. In 1820 there were belonging to Nantucket *seventy-two* whale ships, whose burden together, exceeded *twenty-one thousand, six hundred* tons.

While waiting at Edgarton, she spent her time in holding meetings. She went to Nantucket in a packet ; they started from the wharf about midnight, and the next morning at sunrise arrived at the place of destination, and having never been there before, she was a stranger in a strange land ; but did not remain such long, as the brethren learning that she was on the island sought her out, and gave her a home among them while she staid.

She remained at Nantucket several weeks, and preached at various places, and among the rest, one evening at the *African Chapel;* * in speaking of this meeting, she says,—" The house was well filled with a respectable and attentive congregation, about half of which, were whites. To me, it was a novel scene to look into the galleries, and behold it filled with black singers. There is a flourishing society on the island, made up of colored people. I have been to one of their *Class Meetings,* their leader is a man of color; and it is interesting to witness the deep toned piety, and union of feelings, which seems to prevail among them."

Amid all the sweets of life, Sister Lincoln tasted much of the bitter; and it is truly surprising to see the pains some individuals will take, to render the condition of those around them unhappy. I do not speak in particular reference to Nantucket—I never

* Says her husband,—" Salome was a friend to the colored man, having early manifested that friendship, by uniting herself with an Anti-Slavery Society, while they were in their infancy, and carrying out its principles through life."

was there, but I do not imagine they are worse in that place, *if as bad*, as in many other. Our *church*—Our *minister*—and our *principles*, with many, seems to be of more importance than HOLINESS *of heart !* And what is still worse, this is emphatically so with many, who are professedly pious. How long such a state of things will exist, the Lord only knows !

I repeat it again, and I wish it distinctly understood, that I do not make these remarks particularly in reference to Nantucket. Let not the reader suppose that because Sister Lincoln met with slight opposition there, that the inhabitants are sinners above every other place ; for had she never met with greater trials, her life would have been comparatively free from sorrow ! Then let us not go abroad to find this *abominable wickedness*, but let us come *right home*—to our own *community*—to OUR OWN HEARTS, and if we are free from it ourselves, we are truly fortunate ! May the Lord grant it ! That Salome met with some opposition at Nantucket, is evident from the following extract of a letter written home. Perhaps it might as well be omitted, but as it is short, and expressive of her feel-

10

ings, I will insert it.   She says,—" There appears to be considerable opposition manifested
towards me here, by the ——— church.   But
last evening curiosity or something else,
prompted them to give up their own meeting,
and the *preacher* with *all his people* attended
with us.   However, they manifested no dis-
position to unite, as after preaching not one
of them had any thing to say.   God knows
their motives—I will not judge them.   It was
a severe trial of my faith—but I expected
trials when I started, I expected it would
cost all to gain Heaven, and if I gain it at last,
I shall be richly compensated for all I *have
suffered here !*—I shall then come off conqueror, and more than conqueror through
him that hath loved me, and given himself
for me ! "

Soon after leaving Nantucket she returned
to East Falmouth, and from thence to Wareham, where she staid one week, and held
meetings.   She speaks of the meetings as
not being attended with any particular interest.   From thence she went to Rochester,
and stopped one night, and the next day in
company with Elder Johnston, and Sister
Burgess, went to Rehoboth to attend a four

days meeting. At Rehoboth she met with many of her old friends and acquaintance, it was a pleasant meeting! Such occasions are often rendered delightful, as they give us an opportunity to converse upon the scenes of former days; and the mind is so constituted, that it loves to dwell upon the past as well as the future, especially on such parts as have rendered happiness ;—from Rehoboth she returned home, having now been gone several months.

She remained at home till September, and took several short journeys—preaching Christ wherever she went, both in her own neighborhood and in the adjoining towns. September 12th, she received an invitation to visit several societies in Connecticut; whether she complied with the request or not, the author is unable to say. The following is a copy :—

ROCHESTER, *September* 12, 1832.

"*Dear Sister :*—The brethren in different societies in Connecticut, are anxious to have you come through this section this fall.— Should you come by week after next, you will have an opportunity to ride to the Vermont Conference. If providence opens the way, please to inquire for Br. Baker, *New Hartford;* Ethan Walker, Luther Discall, *Goshen;* and Josiah Brunson, John May, and Thomas Morgan, *Kent.*

> *Respectfully yours, &c.*
>
> ETHAN WALKER."

For the remaining part of this year, and the most of 1833, we shall be able to say but little in relation to the labors of our departed Sister; but probably she spent the time in preaching on the Cape, at Martha's Vineyard, and in the neighborhood of her father's.

In the spring of 1833 she was at Tisbury, where she had been through the winter months: but soon after she left, and never returned, except in one or two instances to visit and attend a camp meeting, which I shall hereafter notice. Her labors on Martha's Vineyard were appreciated, especially at the North Shore. She was respected in every section of the island, and beloved by a large circle of friends.

Passing over the events of 1833, we now come to another important era in her life.— From the last of May 1834, to the middle of August, she preached in Boston, and the adjoining towns, and from the recommendation written by Elder Norris; we learn she was favored with large congregations;* and the approbation of those who heard. She was here at two seasons, first in May, and then again in July; she preached for the Reformed Methodist in Bedford Street, and had made her arrangements to go to Lowell, but as the President of the Conference advised her to defer it till some other time; she put it off. She remained in Boston about two weeks, and preached twelve discourses besides attending other meetings.

After leaving Boston, she made immediate preparation to return to the Cape, to spend the season; her cousin Nancy M. Philips, (now *White*) was expecting to go with her, but providence seemed to order otherwise, as after they had got every thing in readiness, an individual from South Bridgewater came after her to go there and preach; accordingly she relinquished the design of going to the Cape, and returned with him.

East, West, North and South Bridgewater, were formerly one town, situated on the north western boundary of *Plymouth County*.

* See page 42.

10*

It was first divided into four parishes, and afterwards into *four distinct* towns. South Bridgewater retaining the original name, and the others taking the name East, West, and North Bridgewater.

At Bridgewater she preached in a meeting-house belonging to the Universalist. An anecdote respecting her labors there, may not be uninteresting to the reader.

One evening after she had concluded her sermon, she gave an invitation for others who might wish, to make improvement; and accordingly a gentleman who was then under the influence of drink, immediately arose and began to speak. The exhortation would have passed off very well, especially among those unacquainted with him, had not Salome as she was passing out of the house, gone near enough to smell his breath. It was now her turn to exhort, which she did in a faithful manner, and after becoming sober, he was heartily ashamed of his conduct.

From Bridgewater she returned to Boston. This was sometime in the month of July, and she remained there till about the middle of August, when she left to visit the State of Maine. She was in Boston on this visit about six weeks, and the manner she employed her time, may be seen from the following interesting letter written to her consin, Nancy M. Philips. It was dated July 26, 1834, and reads as follows :—

"*Dear Cousin* * * * * * I am as pleasantly situated as I could be in the city; and although there are twenty in the family,* yet I have a room, so that I can be by myself almost as much as though there were no other individual in the house. O Mariah! how I wish you could run in this morning and take a look at my chamber, but as this cannot be, I will tell you how I spend my time. We take breakfast at *seven*. And Br. Norris has kindly supplied me with books from his library, so that after breakfast I am able to spend an hour or two in study and meditation. After this, I work, read, receive company, or make calls, just as circumstances may direct.— Every evening I am engaged, either in class, prayer or preaching meetings, except Saturday. Yesterday I was at Charlestown, and a week from to-day, I expect to go to Malden,

* While in Boston, Salome boarded in the family of Sister Crowell, who kept a boarding house near the Boylston Market.

and spend the Sabbath. * * * * * You speak
in your letter of doubts, respecting your acceptance with God, arising from unfaithfulness, but this does not prove to me that you
have never received a pardon of sin. I well
remember the time when I wholly backslid,
and I have cause to lament my unfaithfulness
even now; yet I cannot doubt that I have
known something of the power of religion.
* * * * Determine to be a christian, and *follow
the Lord* in all things, and then you will find
the way comparatively easy.

Yours affectionately,

SALOME LINCOLN."

One or two evenings before she embarked
for the State of Maine, the city was thrown
into commotion, on account of the burning of
the Ursuline Convent at Charlestown. This
institution was located about two miles west
of the Bunker Hill monument. The ruins
are still to be seen; and it is said the Pope
intends to let them remain, as a witness
against the Protestants, and *to whet the sword
of vengeance,* when he shall have gained the
ascendency over this country. And how
soon this may take place, the Lord only
knows; but this we do know, catholicism is

rapidly spreading—the power of the Pope is daily increasing, and we have just reason to fear that shortly, if not checked, we shall have to *bow our necks* in humble subjection to his HOLINESS, the ROMAN PONTIFF.

But says the reader, " How shall we check it ?" Not by trampling upon their rights, as freemen—plundering their property—ravaging their dwellings—burning their institutions,—and insulting them at every corner of the streets at open noon-day; but if it is done at all, it must be done by the *power of moral suasion;* when that fails, our case is hopeless. And here I could wish, that I had the power to make an appeal that should be heard from the Atlantic to the Pacific, from the northern to the southern boundary, from the centre to the remotest corners of our nation.— Christian ! if you regard your own interest, if you would preserve the liberty of your country inviolate, and if you would save the church from the foul contamination of popery—AWAKE before you find yourselves locked fast in shackles of inquisition !

But do you say there is no cause of *alarm ?*

Let me remind you of the former history of the church ; and then look about you,

and as you witness their wealth, their daily
increase of numbers, and the rapid emigra-
tion from other countries, let it stimulate you
to put forth every exertion to save yourself,
and those around you from this monster,
" *The man of sin !* "   Yet not by physical, but
moral force !   Never act on the principle of
doing evil, that good may come.

The circumstances connected with the
burning of the convent at Charlestown, as
related by Sister Lincoln, in a letter written
to her father,   are briefly these,—* * * * *
" A young lady from the State of New York
sent there by her friends to be educated, was
prevailed upon by the authorities, to take the
veil ; * but soon repenting of this step, she
fled from the convent, and sought the protection of a distant friend.   But not long after
she was visited by the bishop, who promised
her, if she would return with him, she should

* The veil is an article of dress worn by Nuns ; and after
taking it, the individuals are supposed to have dedicated
themselves to perpetual religious seclusion.   When the can-
didate is about to be made a nun, she puts on a religious
habit worn by them, and presents herself before the bishop,
and sings, " The bride of Christ I am !"   She then receives
the veil, &c., and an anathema is denounced against all who
shall attempt to make her break her vows.

be honorably discharged in two or three
weeks. She accordingly returned, and at
the end of three weeks her friends called for
her, but she was not to be seen. The select-
men of the town being applied to, went to the
convent and demanded her. She was at last
brought forward, when she stated that she was
at liberty to go when she pleased, but she chose
to remain. Her appearance was such as led
to the belief that she had been confined in the
cell, and severely tortured, and that she did
not speak the truth. Last night (*Aug.* 11,) a
mob of about 1000 men * from this city went
over at midnight, in disguise, and with lighted
torches searched every cell, and at the same
time set fire to the building. The alarm was
immediately given, and the engine compa-
nies turned out, but when they found what
it was, they refused to play, and together
with the mob, stood and looked on till it was
completely demolished. ''

However bad might have been the character of this institution, it was very unwise, to
take the course they did to destroy it; and
its ruin has done more to build up catholi-

* Probably several thousand.

cism in this country, than all their preaching for the last two centuries.

Had the lightnings of heaven destroyed it, we might have rejoiced; but the same principle that laid that in ruins, would demolish any other institution, when the sentiment advocated clashed with the corrupt principle of their own hearts. And should I be called upon to prove my assertion, I will only refer the reader to the mob of 1842, which assembled around the Bowdoin Square church, while Elder Knapp was lecturing there, and undoubtedly might have leveled it to the ground, had not the city authorities promptly interfered.

Salome in company with Sister Norris, the wife of Elder Norris, and some other friends embarked for Maine on the *fourteenth* of August. They went down in a packet bound for Augusta,* which left Boston about *four* o'clock in the afternoon, and after a voyage of two days, arrived within a few miles of the place of destination. They were intending to have landed at Augusta, but the

---

* Augusta, the capital of Maine, is a flourishing town, situated on the Kennebec river, north east of Portland, and nearly in the centre of the State.

weather proving calm, they were obliged to anchor, and land in the boats at a town a few miles this side. At this place they took the stage and proceeded on to Reedfield.* She stopped at Reedfield several days, and while here preached on Kent's Hill,† to a large congregation. She was solicited to preach there again, but some objection being raised, she declined; but gave out an appointment for a meeting in a village at Fayette; ‡ and when the time arrived, a large congregation assembled, and among them, many of the students, who had followed her down from the hill, so eager were they to hear. She afterwards preached several discourses in the same neighborhood, and once in a grove.

She remained in this section, seven or eight weeks, and while gone, visited besides the towns already noticed, Hallowell, Augusta, Wane, Livermore, Green, Minot, Leeds, &c. &c.

"In these places" (says Elder Norris)

* A town a few miles beyond Augusta.

† That part of Reedfield where the Methodist School is located.

‡ The place where she preached in Fayette, is but a short distance from Kent's Hill.

11

" she was generally well received, she drew out *hundreds*, and in some instances *thousands* to hear her preach ; and she occupied Meeting-houses, School-houses, Town-houses and groves, as the occasion and opportunity seemed to direct. In some of these places her sermons produced much effect, especially in Reedfield, Leeds, Fayette, Wane, and Livermore."

Having closed her visit there she made preparation to return again to Boston, although her friends were very anxious that she should remain longer ; and accordingly with those who accompanied her, she took a packet bound homeward, and after a prosperous voyage, landed safely in her own native state. While returning, it is stated she preached on board the boat, but nothing more definite can be said in relation to her discourse. After arriving at Boston she returned home, where she probably remained during the rest of the season.

Leaving the remaining events of this year, I hasten to close the chapter ; I should be glad if it were in my power, to be still more definite during this period ; although I am sometimes led to think, while reading the memoir of others, that a constant repetition of events, though interesting in themselves render a work of this character dull to the reader, from the *sameness* in style, which must from the nature of the case, unavoidably occur. But notwithstanding this, I should be glad to particularize here, as I am fully satisfied in my own mind, that this was one of the most important periods of her life. But unfortunately as the papers which we have gathered, throw but little light, the reader must remain satisfied at present, * with what I have now in an imperfect manner endeavored to lay before him.

With the close of this, I shall have finished the series of chapters which I have thought proper to head " *The Female Preacher,* " and shall enter upon another event which though not so important in its nature, is equally interesting ; and here I would add, that though I shall not designate her by the title of those chapters, let not the reader gain the impression, that I shall no longer notice her in that

* Should the sale of this edition warrant us in publishing another, many more facts may be added, as we shall have an opportunity of visiting Maine, and many other places where she labored in 1833 and '34.

important relation ; as I have yet several very interesting circumstances to relate.

And now respected reader ! having traced the life of Sister Lincoln thus far, and having learned her trials, the evidence of her high calling, the success which attended her labors, are you not satisfied, whatever may be right or wrong on this subject, that she engaged in this work with pure motives, and with a mind deeply convicted that God had made it her duty. If you are not, any thing further that I could add, will fail of its object, therefore I close the subject.

CHAPTER VII.

THE WIFE.

"Marriage is honorable."—*Paul.*

"Joys serious and sublime,
Such as doth nerve the energies of prayer,
Should swell the bosom—when a maiden's hand,
Filled with life's dewy flowers, girdeth on
That harness, which the MINISTRY OF DEATH
Alone unlooseth, but whose fearful power
May *stamp the sentence* of ETERNITY!"

WHILE marriage is honorable, it is a solemn and interesting rite; and those about engaging in it, should look well to all its relations.

Much grace—much wisdom—and much prayer, is needed by those about entering into a covenant, so solemn that the poet tells us, it is stamped with the *impress of* ETERNITY.— And yet how few there are, especially among the young, who are willing to treat this subject in its proper light.

Franklin, and some other excellent writers, have recommended *early marriage,* as the most productive of happiness; and while I

11*

would recommend candid and prayerful reflection, I would in no wise repudiate this
sentiment, as doubtless one of the principal
causes why so many unhappy unions are
formed, is that they are formed no *earlier* in
life. Early marriages are the most favorable
for the promotion of happiness, from the fact,
that in youth our feelings will more readily as-
similate with the feelings of others.

In selecting a companion, it should be our
aim to select one, whose views—whose feelings—whose temperament—and whose interest, shall correspond with our own! One with
whom we can take sweet intercourse—One
who shall be a companion in health and prosperity—a solace and comforter in sickness—
a partner of our misfortunes, and a sharer of
our joys!

He that marries upon this principle, relying
on the blessing of God, will not fail to add
not only to his own, but the happiness of
those around him. But let the individual
who unites in marriage with another, on any
other principle, remember, that he is preparing for himself a *cup to drink*, which will em-
bitter all the social relations of life.

Sister Lincoln first became acquainted with Elder Mowry sometime in the fall of 1831. She was at that time preaching on Martha's Vineyard, and he was laboring with the Free Will Baptist church at Taunton. And while on one of his pastoral visits, he called at her father's in Raynham. Her cousin, Nancy M. Philips was about writing to her, and as she thought Elder Mowry might sympathize with Salome in her trials, requested him to improve a part of the sheet, which he accordingly did ; but without the most distant idea that the correspondence thus begun, would ever result in a union. The following is an extract from the letter then written :—

RAYNHAM, *Nov. 8th*, 1831.

" *Beloved Sister in Christ :*—Permit one who never beheld your face, to address a few lines to you by way of comfort, while you are upon the same errand of mercy to the human family, as he who is penning these lines :—The *errand of* SALVATION ! O how delightful to carry it to the sons and daughters of apostate Adam ! What a theme of rejoicing to our souls, that we were made the partakers of that principle, which teaches us the importance of denying self—taking up the cross—and following in the paths that lead to heaven! O may we at this time though strangers in the flesh, praise that God in the spirit, who is a spirit, " and seeketh such to worship him ; that it may be done in an acceptable manner." * * * * * Experience has taught me the trials you have to encounter in this vale of tears, but how happy should we be to think that Jesus has *marked* the way *with his blood.* * * * * * O Salome, be faithful in all things, and God will bless you ! study the scriptures—pray much—watch over your own spirit, pray for yourself—pray for Zion ; pray for me—pray for all ! "

Yours, &c.

JUNIA S. MOWRY.

Soon after receiving this, she took occasion to return the following reply :—

TISBURY, *Nov. 27th*, 1831.

Brother Mowry :—I acknowledge with pleasure, the reception of a few lines from you in my cousin's letter, and I now propose to spend the few leisure moments I have, in writing to one whom I can address by the appellation of friend though a stranger in the flesh.

There is a tie that binds the lovers of Jesus together stronger than anything of an earthly nature, and while reading your letter, I felt that it was the language of one who knew how to sympathize with me. * * * * *—Yes, Br. Mowry, I can praise God with you, for the promise we have beyond the grave, of an inheritance that is better than any earthly possession, and that we have an earnest of this inheritence in the present life ; and thank the Lord that the way is the same now, that it was when the apostle counted ALL THINGS *as loss and dross* for the excellency of the knowledge of Christ. I have never repented the sacrifice I have made for the cause of God, and poor souls. There is truly a satisfaction in proclaiming a full and free salvation to the perishing sons and daughters of Adam, and pointing sinners to the lamb of God. * * * * * I will now draw to a close, and if we never meet on earth, may we meet around our father's dazzling throne, there to unite in the praises of HIS *great name.*" * * * *

Yours, &c.

SALOME LINCOLN.

Although these letters passed between them at this time, yet they were not favored with a personal interview, till some months afterwards.

She returned from the Vineyard in the spring of 1832, and while on her visit at home, she attended a meeting held at Whittington village ; * where Elder Mowry had an appointment to preach.   After sermon she made some remarks, and the meeting being concluded, they met and conversed familiarly for a few moments, and then separated ; and from this time till 1835, the year of their marriage, they held but little if any correspondence.

After resigning the pastoral charge of the church at Taunton, Elder Mowry left and went to Tiverton, R. I., and became the Pastor of the Freewill Baptist church in that place, and preached to them one half of the time, and the other half they were destitute. This being the case, and Elder Mowry learning that Sister Lincoln had no particular place of labor, proposed to some of the friends, that she be invited to make them a visit.   The proposition being acceded to, Elder Mowry soon after went into the vicin-

* A village about two miles north of the Court House in Taunton.

ity of Taunton, to attend a protracted meeting, where he found Salome. He informed her of what had transpired at Tiverton, in relation to herself, and she consented to return with him.

" On the way to Tiverton," says Elder Mowry, " our conversation turned on christian *experience in the ministry* — minister's families, and the *choice* of ministers in *selecting their companions for life ;* and at about the conclusion, I remarked, that I trusted when God thought it duty for me to be thus associated, he would provide some one, with a heart and qualifications suited to *my work !* She afterwards told me, that this remark was what first called her mind to the subject of marriage."

While at Tiverton this summer, she boarded in the family of Mr. Peleg Sanford. This was in the year of 1835. Half of the time on the Sabbath she preached in the old meeting-house, belonging to the Baptists, * and the other half wherever opportunity offered ; and during the week she held meetings in

* This meeting-house stood where the new *Freewill Baptist* now stands, not far from Adam's Corner in Little Compton.

that, and in the adjoining sections. At Tiverton she was highly esteemed as a christian,
and her labors as in other places were productive of good. She was made the instrument in the hands of God of several hopeful
conversions, and among the rest was the case
of Br. James Manchester, whose mind at
that time, if not bordering on skepticism, was
in an impenitent state. One evening during
the summer, she preached in a school-house
in the town of Westport, * from the following
text :

"QUENCH *not the spirit.*"—I. *Thes.* v. 19.

Br. Manchester was present. The word in
times past had failed in reaching his heart,
and though his wife who was a professor, felt
a deep anxiety for his salvation, and often exhorted him to seek an interest in Christ, yet
like many others, he manifested no concern
about himself; and when the spirit of God
strove with his conscience, like one of old he
would say, "Go thy way for this time, when
I have a more convenient season I will
call for thee." The word now preached,

* Westport is a town in the South East part of Mass. in
the southern part of Bristol County, South East of Tiverton
and West of Little Compton.

took a deep root in his heart, and he decided on the spot, that he would seek the Lord, while he might be found, and no longer quench his *Holy Spirit*. He went burdened with sin about two weeks, and then found peace in believing, and is now an active member in the church.

Soon after she came to Tiverton, as is frequently the case in such places, it began to be whispered about, that a union was contemplated between herself and Elder Mowry. But in this, as in many other cases where such reports are flying, there was but little ground to build upon, as they contemplated no such event till some months after.

From the following letter written by herself, it would seem she consented to become the wife of Elder Mowry sometime in the month of September 1835 ; * and as it is expressive of her feelings on that subject, I shall take the liberty to present the reader with a brief extract.

RAYNHAM, *Sept.* 28, 1835.

" *Dear Brother in Christ :* In compliance

* It might not have been till later in the fall. I drew the inference from the letter, but as it is of but little importance ; after reading the letter the reader may draw his own inference.

12

with your request, and in accordance with my
own inclination, I have now retired to converse awhile with you, though absent! A
privilege which I highly esteem—that of retiring from the bustle of the world and conversing with friends *far away*. It is sometimes more pleasant, even to think of distant
friends, than to converse with those that are
with us ; but more pleasant still to communi-
cate with those that occupy our thoughts—it
is next to conversing *face to face*. Nothing of
importance has occurred since I saw you.—
I stopped in Taunton the next night, and the
following day came home, where I found my
friends all well. * * * * * You requested me
to write my thoughts when I got home, and
was alone. I am now alone ; but if as I then
understood you, you meant upon the subject
about which we were conversing, I must con-
fess I know not where to begin. But with
regard to some questions which you asked,
and which I did not then answer, I have since
thought you might impute my silence to indifference. But if it would be any satisfaction for you to know, I will acknowledge, that
were I to consult the feelings of my heart,
and then be honest, I suppose I should answer

the question in the *affirmative;* but fearing that my affections were too easily gained, and that you were prompted by pity for my lonely condition more than any other sentiment, I had determined to be guarded in my expressions and keep them locked up in the secret chambers of my own heart—at least for the present; and perhaps it would have been as well if I had not expressed what I have here written. * * * * * I feel that I can submit all to the *will* and *direction* of the Lord ! O that we may be guided by him in all the affairs of life—that whether we spend our days *together* or *apart*, we may spend them to the *glory of* GOD, and be useful to. our fellow creatures ! Pray for me, and pardon this imperfect scrawl ! " * * * * *.

Yours in the Lord,

SALOME LINCOLN.

A few months before her marriage, she again visited Martha's Vineyard to attend a camp-meeting. They had a pleasant voyage, and arrived on the island a little after sunset, and just as the services for the evening were commencing. In the language of the poet it was a

> " Sweet day, so pure, so calm, so bright,
> The bridal of earth and sky ! "

"The place where the meetings were held,"
in her own language, " was a delightful spot,
shaded with large oaks and inclosed with a
circle of tents, upwards of twenty in number.
The scenery was beautiful ; and everything
around seemed to breathe the spirit of devotion ! I felt to say with the poet,"

> "O would HE more of *heaven* bestow,
>   And let the vessel break ;
> And let my ransomed spirit go,
>   To grasp the God I seek !"

Having now been absent from Martha's
Vineyard for nearly two years, she met with
a hearty welcome from many of her former
associates and friends; and although she did
not preach, yet she was very far from being
idle, as she was actively engaged in the tents
in holding circles of prayer. While engaged
in these duties, a lady by the name of Lewis—
now the wife of Edward Luce, was struck
under powerful convictions. She went into
the tent where they were praying, but she
was in so great distress of mind, that she entirely broke up the meeting. She was afterwards converted, and attributes her awakening to the labors of Sister Lincoln. In speaking
further of her visit, she says,—"The meetings

were interesting, and some of them peculiarly
so. We had preaching four times a day,
with prayer-meetings at every interval; and
about *seventy* professed to have submitted to
Christ. The parting scene was heart-rending;
but we parted in hopes of a meeting, where
we shall no more take the parting hand!
About nine o'clock Saturday morning, we left
the island, but the wind was against us, and
after beating about all day, came to anchor in
Tarpaulin Cove, and some of the brethren
went on shore, and after obtaining a place for a
meeting sent word to the other vessels laying
there, so that in a short time we had a large
congregation; and before the meeting closed
six were on their knees begging for mercy.
One of them was the mate of a brig from
New York. At sunrise the next morning, we
again started for home, and landed at four
o'clock in the afternoon of the same day.—
I was exceedingly sick all day, and so were
many other passengers, but I had the peace
of God reigning in my soul."

MARRIAGE TO ELDER MOWRY:—Sometime
in November, Salome left Tiverton and returned home, to make preparation to consummate her union with Elder JUNIA S. MOWRY.

12*

They were married at her father's residence
in Raynham, *December* 2, 1835, by *Elder*
ENOCH SANFORD, pastor of the Congregational
church in that town. In the evening they
held a meeting at the same place, and Elder
Sanford preached. The next day they rode
as far as Rehoboth, where Elder Mowry was
called to attend a funeral, and from thence
proceeded on to his father's in Smithfield,
Rhode Island.

The Sabbath after marriage, they attended
meeting at Greenville, * and Elder Allen †
being unwell, requested Elder Mowry to
preach for him, which he accordingly did in
the forenoon, and after sermon Elder Allen
gave notice that Mrs. Mowry would preach
in the evening. Their marriage was not generally known at Smithfield, and hence when
this notice was given out, it produced considerable excitement. She preached in the
evening to a congregation much larger than
was usual in that place.

* Greenville is a village in the southern part of Smithfield, about three miles and a half North of Smithville Semi-
nary in North Scituate, R. I., and eight miles west of Providence.

† Then Pastor of the First Free Will Baptist church in
Smithfield.

She afterwards preached several times in that vicinity, once or twice in the meeting-house at North Scituate, and for the first church in Smithfield, located at Georgiaville. After concluding their visit, they returned to Tiverton, and commenced the married life, by boarding in the family of Mr. Peleg Sanford.

CHARACTER OF THE WIFE:—I have already in a former chapter noticed her *general* and *religious character*, but to sustain a good character as a husband or wife, implies something more than is generally embraced in either of these ; though I may fail properly to define the difference. To sustain a good character as a wife, implies not only moral purity, but that the individual is qualified to discharge the domestic duties upon which she is called to enter—all the *little* relations connected with household affairs. We have too many trifles, which we class among the *non essentials*. The *little foxes* spoil the vines—*little drops* make up the ocean, and a few *little faults* make a very essential difference in our characters ! But while I make these remarks, I would not be understood to say, that an individual can be entirely free from fault—but so long as we justify them, either in ourselves or others, we are verily guilty.

One of the traits of character which we shall mark in the good wife, is, *order and neatness about her house.* Though an individual may possess every other trait of character that is amiable and lovely, and fails in this one point, she fails properly to discharge her high office.

According to the testimony of others, and especially her husband, Mrs. Mowry possessed this trait of character in a high degree, says he—" Order was a prominent feature of her mind. *Every* thing *had a place*, and every thing was in *its place.*" Another trait which I shall notice in the good wife, is

INDUSTRY.—Sister Mowry as we have already noticed was industrious, through every period of her life, from the cradle to the grave ; and the first year after marriage, besides attending to her other duties, she earned between *thirty* and *forty* dollars, which she expended for furniture. But while she was frugal and industrious, and provided for her own wants, her heart was also open, and she felt deeply for the wants of others. On one occasion after reading a letter which her hus-

band had received from an indigent brother
in the ministry, she was so deeply affected,
that she mentioned his case in the congregation, and called for aid, and by prompt and
persevering exertion, was enabled to render
him assistance. I might go on and multiply
the qualifications of a *good wife*, but as it is
a deviation from the design of this work, I
proceed to notice lastly, that

Affection for her husband, and family, is
another very essential qualification in the
character of the good wife.

Such was the temperament of Mrs. Mowry,
that she made no *pompous display of love*, and
hence to others she often appeared indifferent, when at the same time her feelings glowed
with warmth. To her husband she was an
excellent companion and assistant, and that
she loved him with all the ardor of a wife,
we cannot for a moment doubt, if we may
be permitted to take his testimony, as received from his lips, and from his letters, of
which the following is an extract.

" *My Dear Salome :*—Yours of the 25th and
29th were received yesterday, with all the
heartfelt satisfaction, I trust a *husband delights
in*, from one who is bound to him by ties

more than mortal—even the *silken chords* of affection, and the *spirit of Christ.* * * * * * I can never repay you for that affection which you maifest towards me, in the tokens of *love* and *friendship*, with which your letters and acts abound. You say in your letter; 'I am comforted in your comfort—sorrow in your sorrow,' &c. &c. I could respond to that sentence : — 'True friends are ONE *in soul*, what one has the other enjoys.'"

I have not noticed these traits in the character of Sister Mowry, because I suppose her to be free from fault. Although she possessed the qualifications of a good wife in as high a degree perhaps, as the majority of women; yet "*to err is human.*" And as she was clothed with human nature, it would not be surprising, if she sometimes deviated from the standard of *the perfect wife*.

ENTERS UPON THE DUTIES OF THE WIFE.— Sister Mowry entered upon the discharge of her domestic duties, in the spring after her marriage (1836) in a house belonging to Dea. Borden ; soon after which, she was called to pass through new and unexpected trials, arising out of some difficulty between the Freewill and Christian Baptist societies in

Tiverton. The circumstances are these. The land on which the *parsonage* was built, was given to the Baptist society in Tiverton by a Mr. Job Almy for the use of said society.— Elder Mowry at this time was the regular pastor of the church to whom the property belonged; but Elder Peckham their former pastor continued to occupy the house till his death, when it was advertised *to let* by the Christian Baptists, who had separated themselves from the regular church. As soon as this advertisement appeared, it excited them to action, and Elder Mowry was prevailed upon to take immediate possession of the property which rightfully belonged to them as a society, and accordingly his goods were forthwith moved on to the premises; and for this, acting as he did—agent for the society, he was sued for "*forcible entry.*"

While all this was transpiring at home, Mrs. Mowry was at Raynham, on a visit to to her friends, and when she returned, instead of finding her furniture where she had left it, she found it set up in one small room in the Parish-house — Widow Peckham occupying the remaining part.

The court which set on this case, was held at the *Stone Bridge*, * and after occupying one day in going through the evidence, the case was decided in favor of the Freewill Baptists.

While the court was in session, on being told by one of the by-standers, that perhaps her husband would have to go to jail, she replied, I am going to stay and see how they decide the case, for if he goes to jail I am going too. This anecdote serves to corroborate what we have already stated in relation to her affection for her husband.

Though the combined circumstances attending this case were naturally irritating, yet through the whole she manifested an excellent spirit, and seemed to be willing to make any sacrifice the cause of God required, and had not circumstances forced her husband to be so much from home, leaving increased responsibility devolving upon her ; and had she not been forced to conduct her household affairs in so small a compass, she would have been comparatively happy through the whole of it.

* A village about five miles from the meeting-house, so called from a bridge which runs across from Tiverton to the island of Rhode Island.

BIRTH AND DEATH OF HER CHILD. — Her first child, Mary Elizabeth, was born Nov. 2, 1837, but she was not blessed with its society long, as God in his providence saw fit soon after to take it to himself. God's ways are mysterious. HE gives and HE takes away ; and when perhaps we cannot tell why,—a valid reason is prominent in the mind of the DEITY. I have sometimes thought, that the tender bud is thus early plucked, to guard the fond parent against letting his or her affections entwine too closely around earthly objects, to the neglect of *higher* duties. But to christian parents, when their children are thus taken from them by death, there is a consolation found in the words of Christ : " *Of* SUCH *is the kingdom of* HEAVEN."

This child was never well from birth, and was several times brought so low, that it was thought to be dying. The disease which finally terminated its existence, was the *dropsy*, and after a protracted illness of several months it fell asleep Feb. 5, 1839, leaving its fond parents to mourn its loss.

At the request of Sister Mowry, *Elder* JAMES MC KENZIE, Pastor of the Freewill

Baptist Church at Newport, R. I., * attended
the funeral, and preached a discourse from a
text selected by herself.

"Is it *well* with *thee*? Is it *well* with thy
husband? *Is it well* with the CHILD?—And *she*
answered; *It is well*."—II. *Kings* iv. 26.

She felt the death of her child severely,
yet she manifested christian resignation.—
Says Elder Mc Kenzie—"When I entered
the room, there was no boisterous emotions
of grief, but her looks and language, was expressive of an entire submission to the will of
God."

In a letter afterwards written to her devoted friend Elizabeth Liscom, she says:—
"The sweet little pratler has gone to the
world of spirits, and I shall soon follow!"
But how soon she little realized! We are
often, deeply impressed with the uncertainty
of life, but none know how brief a space of
time, may intervene between them and the
eternal world. I once visited the sick-room
of a friend, when she requested me to sing
the following lines:—and when I see individuals living from day to day, as though there

* Elder Mc Kenzie is now pastor of the Roger Williams,
a Freewill Baptist church in Providence, R. I.

were no *death*—no *judgment*—no ETERNITY
I often think of them.

> " My days, my weeks, my months, my years,
> Fly rapid as the whirling spheres,
>   Around the steady pole ;
> TIME, like the tide, its motion keeps,
> And I must launch thro' boundless deeps,
>   Where endless ages roll.
>
> Long ere the sun has run its round,
> I may be buried under ground,
>   And there in silence rot.
> Alas ! *one hour* may close the scene,
> And ere *twelve months* shall intervene,
>   My NAME *be quite forgot!*
>
> But shall my soul be then extinct,
> And cease to be, or cease to think ?
>   It *cannot—cannot be !*
> Thou ! my IMMORTAL, *cannot die,*
> What wilt thou *do* or whither *fly*
>   When *death shall set you free ?* "

After her marriage, Sister Mowry preached
only occasionally, during the absence of her
husband, or as she went out from home to
visit with him in different places among their
friends.

In the year 1839 she took up her connection with the Reformed Methodist church, of
which she had been a member for a series of
years, and united with the FREEWILL BAPTIST,

at Tiverton. We have now seen her in nearly every relation in life! We have only to witness her through *one more trial*, the *valley* and *shadow* of DEATH, when perhaps we shall be competent to judge of her character, and the motives which governed her actions. This solemn event will be the subject of our next chapter.

CHAPTER VIII.

THE LAST SICKNESS.

" Consult life's silent clock, thy bounding vein,
  Seems it to say—health here has long to reign ?
Hast thou the vigor of thy youth, an eye
  That beams delight, a heart untaught to sigh ?
Yet fear, youth oftentimes healthful and at ease,
Anticipates a day it never sees ! "—*Cowper*.

It oftentimes becomes the duty of the narrator to record events which his feelings would fain prompt him to pass over in silence. We love to dwell upon prosperity—we love to paint the beauties of nature—and trace the hidden springs of happiness ; but to follow death in all his secret windings, is equally painful, both to the writer and reader ; especially when we are called to record the last earthly scenes of a beloved friend !

But says the sacred penman—"It is appointed unto men once to die "—and there is a consolation in knowing, that those of whose virtues we speak, have died in the *triumph*
13*

of faith and are now sweetly sleeping in the arms of Jesus.

It was early evident to the friends of Mrs. Mowry, that the seeds of death were sown in her constitution, and were fast ripening for a premature grave; and yet for a long time they continued to cherish hopes, that by proper care, she might live many years to extend her usefulness in the church, and in the society around her. But alas, how vain are all our expectations! Consumption had fixed its firm, though steady grasp upon her, and was silently, though almost impreceptibly bringing her daily nearer and nearer to the grave.

Consumption is one of the most obstinate diseases with which the skilful physician has to contend. One day the patient seems to be in the enjoyment of health, while on the next he is worn down with disease. It is like the waves of the ocean—*up* and *down*, only each successive wave sinking deeper and deeper, till finally it places its subject forever beyond the reach of hope.— But after all, it is nature's death! So *calm*— so *sweet*, that the poet was led to desire that he might die of the consumption, in order that his friends while they stood around his coffin, viewing his remains, might be led to exclaim, " O how lovely ! "

The disease which terminated the existence of Sister Mowry was a *quick consumption*, which had its origin in a *cancerous humor*, to which she was subject from childhood.

There are several kinds of consumption, and they are as different in their results, as they are in their nature ; for while one leads its subject gently along as described above, other kinds are attended with great mental and bodily distress. Such was the nature of the disorder with which she was afflicted.

After the birth of her second child, March 20, 1841, Mrs. Mowry never regained her health, although some part of the time she was able to keep about the house. They were then living at Warwick, R. I. ; * Elder Mowry having ended his labors with the church at Tiverton, Nov. 1840, and taken the pastoral charge of the Central Freewill Baptist church in the village of Aponaug. Miss Nancy Manchester, the present wife of Elder Mowry, was with her, and took charge of her

* Warwick is in Kent's County, about ten miles South of Providence.

domestic affairs through the remaining part of her life.

PREACHED HER LAST SERMON.—It is often the case that individuals think much of the last acts, or the last words of a departed friend; and especially if they were called to take a prominent part in public. The last notice we have of Mrs Mowry's preaching, is contained in a letter written to a friend, and dated April 5, 1840. In this letter she says:—"To-day, as we were disappointed of a minister, I have tried to preach. I have not attempted it before, for several months, but I had a good time in speaking from these words:—

"If any man be in CHRIST, *he is a new creature*—I. Cor. v. 17.

After I had done two young men recently converted, brought in their testimony, which was to the point." After this sermon, she probably never took a text in the public congregation, although she may have been engaged in conferences, where, as Eld. Whittemore tells us her talents shown with peculiar lustre.

Subsequent to the twentieth of May, 1841, she never left her room, only as she was

carried in the arms of her husband ; and for
about nine weeks previous to her death, she
had constant watchers, and every means that
could be suggested to the minds of her friends,
was resorted to, in order to secure her recovery ; but all in vain, as from that time she
rapidly declined. In a letter dated July 6th,
her husband says :—

"Salome has suffered very much. She
often speaks of it. She has been singularly
affected — long continued — and still it looks
dark. Saturday I went to Providence and
called upon Dr. Richardson, (Botanic, *)—he
comes again to-day—she is so low he scarcely
knows what to say of her, or the complaint.
He gave her medicine, but she takes only a
little at a time, and it distresses her exceedingly. In some respects she appears better,
in others not,—on the whole is more comfort-
able than when Brother Whittemore was up.
I have still some little hopes of her recovery,
but time alone can determine."

The last two weeks before her death, she
conversed but little, owing to the peculiar state

---

* She had a Botanic Physician at her own request. She
seemed to have confidence that they could restore her to
health.

of her mind produced by her disorder. Her mind, though in health strong, in sickness seemed to be broken; but as death drew nearer, she was calm and resigned, and appeared more rational, and seemed more like herself.

LAST HOURS AND DEATH.—A few days before her death, Elder Joseph Whittemore, from Tiverton, called to see her. He says— "She appeared to know me, and would converse rational about the people of Tiverton. She expressed a *strong desire* for the prosperity of the church there; and when asked in relation to her own feelings, she said she was sensible, she should never get well, and felt *resigned* to the will of God. She also remarked, that in prospect of death, she felt more calm then she ever expected; although if it was the will of God, she should like to regain her health; but not so much on her own account, as on the account of her husband and child."

On another occasion she remarked to her husband, that she did not have that lively, animated state of feelings which she desired, and had not for some months past,—but felt firm, and could rely on Christ as her Savior.

At another time she said—"Christ is my only hope of salvation, *on which I lean my all!*"

When asked about her burial, she replied—"I have thought much of it, and should prefer to be laid with my child at Tiverton."

During the last few hours of her life, she seemed to lie almost entirely senseless, and in so great a bodily distress, that her groans were heard in the street ; and at the same time, she was in a state of mental *aberration.* Her *bodily suffering* during this period was doubtless *beyond conception*, and it would not be surprising if under these circumstances, she often appeared indifferent, as to her situation. She remained in this state until about *four o'clock* Wednesday afternoon, *July* 21, 1841, *when she departed this life to be with* JESUS.

She is now free from pain and sorrow—her trials are at an end, and she is reaping a rich reward for all her toils, in the *Kingdom of Heaven!* "Blessed are the dead that die in the Lord!"

Her earthly pilgrimage is now closed !— that voice which once sounded the news of salvation so earnestly, will be heard no more! Her tongue is silenced in death !—Her eyes which beamed with intelligence are closed—and her mortal has put on immortality! And while her body sleeps in the cold arms of death — her spirit freed from its earthly tenement, has gone to inhabit the *regions of bliss*—or in the language of the poet :

" She has gone to the grave—but we will not deplore her,
  Though sorrow and darkness encompass the tomb:
The SAVIOR *has passed through its portals* before her,
  And the *lamp of his love*, is her guide through the gloom.

She has gone to the grave, but 'twere wrong to deplore her,
  When God was her ransom, her guardian and guide ;
He *gave her*—and *took her*—and soon will *restore* her,
  Where DEATH *hath no sting*, since the *Savior hath died.*"

At the time of her death, Mrs. Mowry was a member of the Freewill Baptist church at Warwick. This is the second time within a few years, that that church, in the providence of God has been called to follow the remains of their pastor's companion to the grave.*— God is speaking by these events to the church at Warwick, reminding them of the importance of working while the *day lasts*, remembering that the night of death will soon come, when there will be no more opportunity.

By the death of Sister Mowry, God also

* Elder Benjamin Phelon, while he had the charge of that church buried a wife and child.

speaks to the surviving friends, and especially to those, who have so often heard her voice in prayer and exhortation, and have not profited by her admonitions, but who are yet without Christ; To *you* my *dear friends!* God is speaking by this providence in *thunder tones,* saying, " be ye also ready!"—To her relatives and numerous circle of *pious* friends SHE *soon will* speak with the voice of an AN-GEL, in *tones* of *consolation;* "Friends, JESUS *calls come home!*"

Among a large circle of *relatives* and *friends,* Mrs. Mowry left one child; * then *four months* old—a bright black eyed little girl! Though possessing naturally a delicate constitution, yet by the tender care of her parent and guardian, she may live many years, to follow in the footsteps of her mother,—an ornament in society—a pillar in the church, and useful to all around her!

FUNERAL OF MRS. MOWRY:—The circumstances connected with the funeral of Mrs. Mowry, were *solemnly sublime!* And as probably but very few of my readers, have ever been called to witness anything like it,

---

* Amy Mowry, the second daughter of Salome, was born March 20, 1841.

they will pardon me, if I should wander from that *deep solemnity* which should ever grace these solemn occasions. There is that connected with the services performed at the funeral of our friends, which always has a tendency to touch the feelings, and draw out the sympathy of our natures ! The assembling of the relatives and friends together— The touching appeals of the devout minister of Christ—The appendages of the dead—the *pall*, the *bier*, the *shroud*, the *coffin*—and then the solemn tones of the *plaintive bell*, as the procession moves *slowly* onward to the grave ;— all, all conspire to melt our hearts, and make us weep ! But to witness *a burial at* MIDNIGHT ! to lay our friends down, as in the language of the poet,

" By the struggling *moonbeams'* misty light, "

far surpasses this, and everything else, within the limits of discription !

The funeral services of the deceased were commenced at the residence of Elder Mowry in Warwick, Friday morning, July 23. At *eight* o'clock, Eld. Fifeild, a Methodist minister stationed on the circuit, made a prayer at the house, after which they moved in pro-

cession to East Greenwich.* They arrived
there about *ten* o'clock A. M. when the remains were taken from the hearse, and placed
on board a sloop, waiting for the purpose of
conveying them to Tiverton. Says Elder
Mowry:—

"The hours of this day rolled heavily."

They were expecting to have arrived at
Tiverton by four o'clock in the afternoon,
but the day proving exceedingly calm, they
made but little progress; and it was past
sunset before they arrived at the Stone Bridge,
seven miles from the place of interment.—
Tiverton and Little Compton are separated
from the island of Rhode Island † by the
Eastern Passage of the Narraganset Bay,
and the only connecting link is the Stone
Bridge, just referred to. The tide which
comes in from the ocean, through this passage to Mount Hope Bay, passes and re-pas-

* East Greenwich lies South of Warwick, and the place
where they took the sloop is about three miles from Aponaug.

† The island of *Rhode Island*, from which the State de-
rives its name, is situated in the Narraganset Bay. It is
one of the most delightful spots I have ever visited, and from
its fancied resemblance to the garden of Eden, it has sometimes been called the *Eden of America*.

ses with considerable rapidity, so that a vessel wishing to go through the drawer, must
pass in the direction of the tide.

They were expecting to have landed four
miles below the bridge, and within about the
same distance of the place of burial, where
some of the friends with carriages were to
meet them. But when they arrived at the
bridge the tide had just turned against them,
and they were forced, either to land or wait
six hours longer; and it being in mid-summer,
they concluded to land.

The scene which is now to follow, surpasses description—the pen of the poet would
fail to paint it!—Having obtained a sufficient
number of carriages, the *procession* again
moved forward—and between *twelve* and *one*
o'clock, Saturday morning, July 24th, they
arrived at the place of burial; and between
ONE and TWO—at "DEAD *of* NIGHT"—while
a solemn stillness reigned around,—they LAID
HER DOWN, IN THE SILENT GRAVE — "IN
Death's cold arms to sleep ! "

> "No more with us, HER *tuneful* voice,
>   The hymns of praise shall swell;
> No more her *cheerful heart rejoice*,
>   To hear the SABBATH BELL!"

Early in the forenoon of the same day, they again assembled at the house of Elder Whittemore, and after reading a portion of Scripture, he offered up a *solemn* and *devout* prayer to God!

The room where they were assembled, was the same in which she had lived—It was painted by her own hands—and the same furniture stood in it, which had been used by herself; and as simple as they appear in themselves, these circumstances had a tendency to render the scene doubly solemn and interesting!

After the services were ended, they retired to the sloop—and returned to Warwick.

The next day being the Sabbath, two funeral discourses were preached to the church at Aponaug; one in the forenoon by Elder Martin Cheney, a Freewill Baptist minister from Olneyville, * and the other by Elder Waterman a Congregationalist.† Elder Che-

---

* Olneyville, is a village, partly in Johnston and partly in North Providence, R. I. Elder Cheney's meeting-house is in Johnston, about two miles from the Court-house, Providence.

†, I should be exceedingly glad to present the reader with an outline of Elder Waterman's discourse, but not having the means, it is out of my power.

ney's text was from the words of the Apostle contained in the first of Thessalonians :—

" But I would not have you to be *ignorant* brethren, *concerning them which are* ASLEEP, that ye *sorrow* not, even as others *which have* no HOPE."—I. *Thess.* iv. 13.

A few Sabbaths after Elder Whittemore preached a funeral discourse to the church at Tiverton, laying before them the life and character of the deceased ; the words of his text were as follows :—

" That ye be not *slothful*, but *followers of them*, WHO through *faith* and *patience* INHERIT THE PROMISE."—*Hebrews* vi. 12.

In his exordium he remarked, — " It is the duty of the *living*, to *remember* THOSE who *have died* in CHRIST, and to COPY *their example* as far as it was good—and in discussing this subject, I shall show :—

I. THE ADVANTAGE OF REMEMBERING SUCH AS THROUGH FAITH AND PATIENCE INHERIT THE PROMISE.

II. MENTION A FEW THINGS IN THE CHARACTER OF THE DECEASED WORTHY OF REMEMBRANCE.

Besides these sermons, Elder Whittemore also wrote an obituary notice, which was

published in the Morning Star.* He was per-
sonally acquainted with her, having lived in
their family several months ; and having many
other superior advantages over the author,
I can only regret that his other duties pre-
cluded him from the privilege of transmitting
to the world, the memoir of her, who so
richly deserves a place, not only in our affections but also in our *memory*.

She has left us, and gone to the silent
abode of the dead, where,

> " The storm that wrecks the winter skies,
> No more disturbs her deep repose,
> Than summer evening's latest sigh,
> That shuts the rose !

But while we mourn her loss, we mourn
not as those destitute of a hope in CHRIST,
who is the resurrection ; for when life's flickering lamp ceased to burn, her spirit guided by
angels, soared away to the mansions of ETER-
NAL REST—there to unite with those kindred
spirits who had gone before her !—And at
the resurrection of the saints she will stand
in her lot and place !

The following beautiful " Requiem," taken
from the Philadelphia Gazette, and supposed

* The Morning Star is a religious paper published by the
Freewill Baptists at Dover, New Hampshire.

to be the production of the editor, composed
on the death of his accomplished lady, was
handed to me by Elder Mowry for insertion.

> " I see thee still!
> Remembrance faithful to her trust,
> Calls thee in beauty from the dust;
> Thou comest in the morning light—
> Thou'rt with me through the gloomy night;
> In dreams I meet thee, as of old,
> Then thy soft arms, my neck enfold,
> And thy sweet voice is in my ear;
> In every scene to memory dear,
>   I *see thee* still!
>
> I see thee still!
> Here was thy summer noon's retreat,
> This was thy favorite fireside seat;
> This was thy *chamber*, where each day
> I sat and watched thy *sad decay;*
> Here on *this bed* thou last did lie,
> Here on *this pillow, thou didst* DIE!
> *Dark hour!* once more its woes unfold—
> As then I saw thee *pale* and *cold,*
>   *I see thee still!*
>
> I see thee still!
> Thou art not in the tomb confined,
> Death cannot claim the IMMORTAL MIND!
> Let earth close o'er its sacred trust,
> Yet *goodness* DIES *not in the dust.*
> THEE oh beloved! 'tis not thee,
> Beneath the coffin's lid I see,
> Thou to a *fairer land art gone*—
> There let me hope—my journey done
>   *To see thee still!*"

Mrs. Mowry was buried near her child, in the yard a few rods north of the Stone meeting-house belonging to the Freewill Baptists in Tiverton. The grave is situated in the southern part of the yard, near the gate. It is marked by two white marble slabs, on which is inscribed the following appropriate words.:—

In Memory

OF

SALOME MOWRY,

THE WIFE OF

ELDER JUNIA S. MOWRY,

Who died July 21, 1841, in the 34th year of her age.

She spent more than five years as a public laborer in various places; mostly in the *south-eastern* part of *Massachusetts.*

And now Dear Reader !—after having thus endeavored to lay before you in a faithful manner, the life and character of Mrs. Mowry, permit me to take a kind and affectionate leave of you, by requesting that you will strive to profit by her example—to imitate her virtues—and live here in such a manner, that when death shall draw nigh, like the apostle Paul you may have it to say,—"I have *fought a good fight*, I have *finished my course*, I have *kept the faith :* Henceforth there is *laid up for me*, A CROWN OF RIGHTEOUSNESS, which the Lord the RIGHTEOUS JUDGE shall give me at that day : and not to me only, but unto ALL *them also that love his appearing*." May the Lord grant it ! and may you and I, so spend our days, that when with her we shall be called to stand at the judgment seat of Christ, we may be prepared to render up our account "with *joy, and not with grief*."

ERRATA. Page 46, 21st line; for "will never," read "*shall* never."—39th page, line 15, read "far more *exceeding* and eternal," &c.—Page 111, line 4, for 1843, read 1833.

American Women: Images and Realities
An Arno Press Collection

[Adams, Charles F., editor]. **Correspondence between John Adams and Mercy Warren Relating to Her "History of the American Revolution," July-August, 1807.** With a new appendix of specimen pages from the **"History."** 1878.

[Arling], Emanie Sachs. **"The Terrible Siren": Victoria Woodhull, (1838-1927).** 1928.

Beard, Mary Ritter. **Woman's Work in Municipalities.** 1915.

Blanc, Madame [Marie Therese de Solms]. **The Condition of Woman in the United States.** 1895.

Bradford, Gamaliel. **Wives.** 1925.

Branagan, Thomas. **The Excellency of the Female Character Vindicated.** 1808.

Breckinridge, Sophonisba P. **Women in the Twentieth Century.** 1933.

Campbell, Helen. **Women Wage-Earners.** 1893.

Coolidge, Mary Roberts. **Why Women Are So.** 1912.

Dall, Caroline H. **The College, the Market, and the Court.** 1867.

[D'Arusmont], Frances Wright. **Life, Letters and Lectures: 1834, 1844.** 1972.

Davis, Almond H. **The Female Preacher, or Memoir of Salome Lincoln.** 1843.

Ellington, George. **The Women of New York.** 1869.

Farnham, Eliza W[oodson]. **Life in Prairie Land.** 1846.

Gage, Matilda Joslyn. **Woman, Church and State.** [1900].

Gilman, Charlotte Perkins. **The Living of Charlotte Perkins Gilman.** 1935.

Groves, Ernest R. **The American Woman.** 1944.

Hale, [Sarah J.] **Manners; or, Happy Homes and Good Society All the Year Round.** 1868.

Higginson, Thomas Wentworth. **Women and the Alphabet.** 1900.

Howe, Julia Ward, editor. **Sex and Education.** 1874.

La Follette, Suzanne. **Concerning Women.** 1926.

Leslie, Eliza . **Miss Leslie's Behaviour Book: A Guide and Manual for Ladies.** 1859.

Livermore, Mary A. **My Story of the War.** 1889.

Logan, Mrs. John A. (Mary S.) **The Part Taken By Women in American History.** 1912.

McGuire, Judith W. (A Lady of Virginia). **Diary of a Southern Refugee, During the War.** 1867.

Mann, Herman . **The Female Review: Life of Deborah Sampson.** 1866.

Meyer, Annie Nathan, editor. **Woman's Work in America.** 1891.

Myerson, Abraham. **The Nervous Housewife.** 1927.

Parsons, Elsie Clews. **The Old-Fashioned Woman.** 1913.

Porter, Sarah Harvey. **The Life and Times of Anne Royall.** 1909.

Pruette, Lorine. **Women and Leisure: A Study of Social Waste.** 1924.

Salmon, Lucy Maynard. **Domestic Service.** 1897.

Sanger, William W. **The History of Prostitution.** 1859.

Smith, Julia E. **Abby Smith and Her Cows.** 1877.

Spencer, Anna Garlin. **Woman's Share in Social Culture.** 1913.

Sprague, William Forrest. **Women and the West.** 1940.

Stanton, Elizabeth Cady. **The Woman's Bible** Parts I and II. 1895/1898.

Stewart, Mrs. Eliza Daniel . **Memories of the Crusade.** 1889.

Todd, John. **Woman's Rights.** 1867. [Dodge, Mary A.] (Gail Hamilton, pseud.) **Woman's Wrongs.** 1868.

Van Rensselaer, Mrs. John King. **The Goede Vrouw of Mana-ha-ta.** 1898.

Velazquez, Loreta Janeta. **The Woman in Battle.** 1876.

Vietor, Agnes C., editor. **A Woman's Quest: The Life of Marie E. Zakrzewska, M.D.** 1924.

Woodbury , Helen L. Sumner. **Equal Suffrage.** 1909.

Young, Ann Eliza. **Wife No. 19.** 1875.